中外文化精萃丛书

半坡母系社会

赵文艺 宋 澎 编著

Banpo matriarchal society

西安半坡博物馆供稿

半坡博物馆大门

半坡遗址外景

尖底瓶

彩陶壶

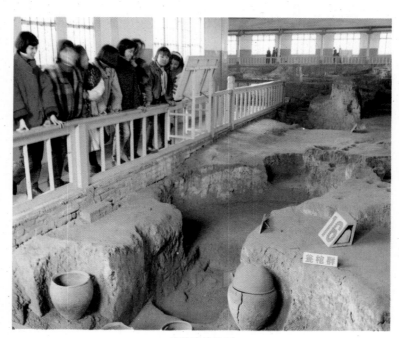

半坡遗址展厅

单体鱼盆

人面网纹盆

李瑞环、张勃兴参观半坡,赵文艺陪同讲解。

台湾著名女作家琼瑶偕夫平鑫涛参观半坡,自左起平鑫涛、琼瑶、相阳、何克敬、赵文
艺、刘云辉。

目　录

前　言

　　半坡遗址，位于西安市东郊浐河东岸的第二级台地上，大约在距今六千七百年以前，在这里生活着一群人，他们日出而作、日落而息，过着一种以女性为中心的生活，他们就是著名的半坡人，他们所处的时代正是原始社会母系氏族公社的鼎盛时期。

　　斗转星移，苍海桑田，几千年过去了，半坡人连同他们所创造的一切都埋没在荒芜的杂草、瓦砾之中，后世生长在此的人们也丝毫不知道中华民族的祖先曾经在这里辛勤劳动，并创造出了辉煌灿烂的文化，只有到了人民当家作主的新社会，这一人类的宝贵财富才得以重见天日。一九五三年，半坡遗址一经发现，立即受到党和人民政府的高度重视，在陈毅同志的亲切关怀下，经过考古工作者们三年五次大规模科学发掘，共发掘文物近万件，遗址面积达一万多平方米，占遗址总面积的五分之一。并且在一九五八年建成了我国第一座新石器时代的遗址性博物馆，也就是举世闻名的西安半坡博物馆。

　　《半坡母系社会》主要以地下发掘出来的遗迹、遗物为依据，并参考民族学的研究成果，对半坡人的生产、生活、意识形态和社会组织结构等进行分析、探讨而编写的，力图以通俗的形式来普及氏族公社的知识，由于水平有限，其中难免有疏漏之处，务请多加批评指正。

半坡人的生活环境

人类要生存,首先要有一个适宜的生活环境,半坡人之所以能够在人类历史上写下辉煌的篇章,创造出璀璨的原始文化,离不开他们同自然界艰苦卓绝的斗争,同时,在很大程度上得利于黄河流域优良的自然环境。

陕西位于黄河中下游流域,境内有渭河横贯而过,渭河两岸支流密布,土地肥沃,史称八百里秦川,自古就是人类生息繁衍的好地方,也是著名的仰韶文化的发祥地。

凡是到过半坡博物馆的人都会记得,在参观完分布于两侧的展室之后,到达院落尽头,会发现地势突然陡峻,整齐的台阶展布在面前,高约八米,游人只有拾级而上才能到达六、七千年前半坡人居住过的地方,而您是否想到,这台阶正是半坡先民赖以生存的浐河的古河岸,称作阶地陡坎。

为什么半坡人要选择一个临近陡坡的地方生活呢?

原来,生存离不开水,但原始人还不会凿井取水,所以,半坡氏族公社时期的人们往往将自己的栖息之所选择在那些土地肥美、距水源近,地势较高又可以避免水患的靠近河流的阶地之上。

浐河发源于秦岭北麓,由南而北地注入渭河,白鹿原和长乐坡之间的低洼地带,便是古代浐河河床的宽度,根据浐河流砂堆积情况,当时浐河的水量是很大的,同样,渭河及其支流灞河的水量也比现在多,而且非常清澈。浐河与灞河进入平原以后变得开阔,在平水季节,浐河、灞河与渭河的水,虽因季节的变化有涨有落,但总体上水势平缓,并不像现在这样暴涨暴落,丰盈的河水,不时溢出,致使河畔有许多湖沼分布,半坡人由于住在沪河边上所以用水不愁。由出土的大量鱼骨以及食鱼为主的貉骨骼的发现,说明沪河里曾滋长着大量的鱼类,此外,还在遗址中发现了大量的螺蛳壳、蚌壳,这些都说明当时沪河不仅供给半坡人生活用水而且还是一个天然的水产基地。

半坡遗址的东边紧靠白鹿原,南接终南山,六千多年以前,那里生长着茂密的原始森林,森林中出没的是各种各样的飞禽走兽。原来,经过我国科学工作者对半坡遗址进行土壤孢子花粉研究,发现了生长在半坡的草类植物有蒿、藜、禾草、葎草等,树木则有柳、胡桃、鹅耳枥、栎、榆和柿等,还发现了只适宜在亚热带生存的铁杉的孢子花粉,同时,发现了不少动物骨骼的残片,如猪、狗、牛、羊、马、鸡、雕、獐、鹿、竹鼠、狐、狸、獾、貉、兔等,其中獐和中华竹鼠的碎骨较多。而獐是今天生长在长江中下游地区的动物,竹鼠与竹林伴生,竹子在我国分布的地界是黄河中下游以南的地区,由这些可推知,半坡人生活期间的气候比现在要温暖湿润,与今天的陕南汉中相类似,当时年平均气温比现在要高出4℃,茂密的森林和出没其间的野兽,为半坡人提供了一个极好的采集和狩猎之地,半坡遗址的北面则是一望无际的渭河平原,是人类从事原始农业的理想场所。

半坡人的自然环境

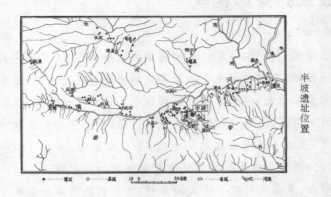

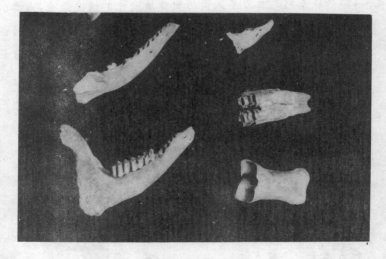

兽类骨骼

　　总之，整个环境依山傍水，气候宜人，非常有利于原始人的定居生活，半坡先民就是在这样一个环境下，依靠勤劳的双手，开垦了富饶的土地，开拓了远古的农业。

半坡人的身形相貌

　　据学者们研究,半坡人属南方蒙古人种,与中国华南人的体质特征接近,是直接继承了山顶洞人的血统发展而来的,是中华民族的直系祖先,其肤色应为我国黄色人种祖先的代表,他们那高而前突的颧骨,从内面凹进的铲状门齿,显示了黄色人种典型的特征,半坡人还有着高高的脑门,平直的鼻部,厚度适中的嘴唇,总之,既有北方人的特征又有着南方人的一些特点。

　　那么,身高呢?关于古人的身长,在我国民间曾流传有古人体躯高大的传说,如:八尺之躯、身高丈二等等,但这并不符合事实,如果联系到二百万年人类历史体质变化的情况来看,人类的身长并非由高变低,而是由低逐渐升高。从已得的化石材料证明,人类在二百多万年前刚刚由古猿跨入人类门楣的时候,身长约在130厘米左右;至五十万年前的北京人时代,身长只有150～160厘米;而半坡人呢,根据半坡遗址中发现的大量人骨分析,身高为170厘米左右,等同于今天人类平均身长,同时,半坡人的脑容量为1376毫升,和现代人的脑容量——1400毫升已相差无几,半坡人已具备了与现代人相等发达的智力,因此,人类学家指出,半坡人与现代人属于一个智人种。

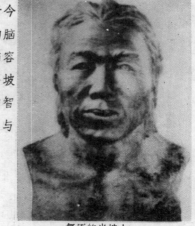

复原的半坡人

半坡氏族的农业生产及家畜饲养

半坡人从事农业生产,有着得天独厚的自然环境和地理条件,六千年前的半坡地区比现在温暖湿润,有森林、平原、沼泽和河流,其中水域出产鱼类,在这种环境中,既有采集、渔猎之便,又有农耕之利,当然,由于当时还没有人工水利设施,人们只能靠天吃饭,从事的是旱地种植。

半坡遗址中出土的农作物主要是粟,人们在一个陶罐里发现了粟籽,粟即谷子,去皮后又称小米,由于粟有种种优点如:耐干旱,适于生长在北方干旱的黄土地带;生产技术简单;收获量大;成熟期短;久藏不坏因而使其成为当时我国北方主要的粮食作物。

那么,粟的来源呢?原来,在人类的早期,共同的劳动和生活将他们组结在一起,自然分工决定了男子从事狩猎、捕鱼等重体力劳动,而妇女则长期从事采集,妇女在从事采集的过程中,逐渐掌握了植物生长的规律,于是就将狗尾草(又称莠、狐尾草)加以驯化,使其成为人工栽培作物——粟。

在半坡遗址中发现粟,充分说明了我国是最早种植粟的国家,而且,也是世界上农业发明最早的国家之一。

粟的出现,就使人类的定居生活成为可能。那么,半坡人是如何种植谷子的呢?从民族学资料来看,我国的独龙族是先将树木砍倒,晒干后焚烧,然后在布满灰土的地表上漫撒粟籽,并用竹扫帚扫一遍,等降雨后就萌芽了,不翻地、不中耕,但要看护好,秋后进行摘穗,整个生产过程并不复杂。从半坡出土的数量很多的砍伐器和石斧来看,人们也是采用火耕的方法开垦土地。人们首先用石斧来砍倒树木杂草,放火焚烧,草木变成天然肥

储存粮食的小陶罐

料,耕地也就被开垦出来了。他们所使用的石斧是经过了一个发展过程,石斧多以比较坚硬的玄武岩为原料,有早、晚期之分,早期的石斧没有钻孔,使用时直接夹在一个劈开的木柄之间,用绳子绑起来即可。这显然不能使木柄牢固,后来发明的钻孔石斧克服了这一弊病,不仅提高了生产的效率,而且使其本身成为一件十分精美的工艺品,虽然人们发明了有钻孔的石斧,但是可以想象,用石斧来砍倒树木的效率仍然是很低的,尽管如此,在金属工具问世以前,石器仍是最主要的生产工具,不论是砍倒树木,开辟耕地,或建造房屋等方面都是必不可少的。它陪伴了人们上百万年之久,经历了考古学上的"石器时代",当然,半坡氏族从事火耕地也可能采用另外的方法,例如像北美易洛魁人那样第一年先由男子们把树皮从巨大的树干上剥下,使树木枯萎,到下一年,再将这些树木烧去。半坡人起初只是砍伐村子附近的林地,久而久之才渐渐向外处开垦。

比较落后的火耕地种植了一年,为了补充地力,便于作物生长,必须进行翻地,才可以继续种植。翻地的工具是石铲,类似于今天的铁锨,除石制的外,还有用兽的肩胛骨作成的骨铲,也一定有类似木耒的木质工具,但是由于时间太久,已经不复存在了。然后,再播撒种子,播种之后,半坡人用石锄来盖土,石锄就类似于我们今天的鹤嘴锄,这种石锄一般是打制的,头部扁尖或扁圆,锄身略窄,一般是安在鹤嘴木柄上使用,还可用来锄草。

半坡时期禽兽种类很多,有田鼠、竹鼠、羊、马、兔和各种鸟类,它们出没于森林、沼泽之中,对农作物是一个严重威胁,为了保住粮食,到了谷子快成熟的时节,就有人住在地里看守,用狩猎的方法捕杀动物。

辛苦劳动的人们终于迎来了金色的秋天,到了收割时节,人们用石刀、陶刀来收获自己的劳动果实,石刀,通常为两侧缺口形式,人们可以在两个缺口间拴一绳套,在手握时将大拇指插入绳套中,这样不易脱落,使用时,以刀刃切断粟杆。到了半坡晚期,人们还发明了安柄的石镰,人们收割时不收秸,只收穗,这同他们那种原始的刀耕火种的耕作方法是分不开的,粟秸被丢在地里,春播时放火焚烧,以补充地力。

半坡人的粮食加工方法可以说已经达到了

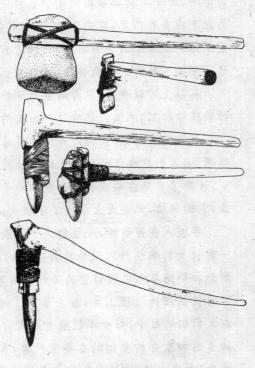

石制工具复原图

1 斧 2 4 锛 3 5 锄

一定水平，遗址中发现了石磨盘和石磨棒，使用的时候，就是将谷物放在石磨盘上，手执石磨棒碾磨，这样可以将谷物去皮或碾碎。当时的加工工具是非常原始、简陋的，但是比半

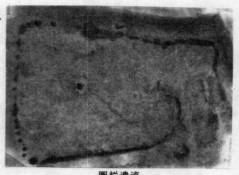

圈栏遗迹

坡早一、两千年的裴李岗文化却已经使用又大又精致的石磨盘，而且下面多有四足，这是为什么呢？其实，从民族学的资料来看，最原始的加工工具是石磨盘，之后才有了石杵和木臼，由于半坡已经应用了较为进步的杵臼，石磨盘也就退居到次要地位了。

从以上可以看出，从开辟耕地到松土下种，作物成熟后再进行收获和加工，半坡人已有了一整套的农业生产经验。

半坡氏族时期，人们还开始了蔬菜的种植，在一个陶制的储藏罐里，人们发现了已经碳化的蔬菜种子，这些标本经过科学鉴定，证明了它是白菜或芥菜一类的种子，蔬菜是一种很好的副食品，它的种植，无疑大大丰富了半坡人的物质生活。

半坡人在劳动时，采取的是一种集体协作的方式，人们是以一种极大的热情投入到生产过程中的，当时，象砍伐树木、开垦耕地和烧除草木等较繁重的工作多由男子担任，而在播种之后，经常性的田间管理工作，就全落到了妇女们的身上，这个时期，在人们的心目中，妇女不但能生产人的自身，而且是人能得以维持生活和生存的食物的主要生产者，有些氏族部落就将妇女推崇为"生产之神"、"地母"，这也是构成母系氏族社会的社会经济形态的一个重要特征。

考古工作者在发掘遗址的过程中还发现了两座饲养家畜的圈栏遗迹,复原起来为栅栏式的圈栏,并发现了猪、狗、牛、羊、马、鸡六种动物的骨骼,据动物驯养史专家的研究,可以确知的家畜当时只有猪和狗两种,牛、羊、马、鸡四种动物估计正在驯养之中。

　　在遗址中发现的大量猪骨多为幼猪骨骼,这说明由于饲养方式不当致使猪大批死亡,或是由于生活条件艰苦,人们不得不杀掉幼猪充饥。

　　家畜的饲养是随着长期的定居生活而发展起来的,可想而知,随着定居生活的出现,人们的食物来源渐趋稳定,狩猎而得的动物不仅供给食用,而且有时会出现剩余,这样,人们便把食余的动物想法养起来,以便来日食用。于是一个新的经济部门——家畜饲养便随之产生了。

狩猎、捕鱼与采集及共食之风

狩猎经济在半坡人的生活中占有相当重要的地位,它不仅供给人们肉食,它还供给食物以外的其它生活方面所需要的用品,如皮毛、骨角和油脂之类,当时在人们居住区的附近除了草地和沼泽之外,还有茂密的丛林,其中生长着相当繁多的游食动物,从遗址中发现的大量狩猎动物骨骼来看,有斑鹿、水鹿、竹鼠、貉、獾、狐狸、兔和鹏鸟等,其中又以斑鹿的骨骼为最多,这也许是由于斑鹿性情温驯,所以易于捕捉的缘故罢。

狩猎活动是集体进行的,狩猎时,男人们结队出行,由富有经验的猎手领队,狩猎的工具有弓箭、石球、石矛等。

弓箭是当时人们的主要狩猎工具,它具有射程远、射速快、推进力大、准确度高、杀伤力强等特点,是最有效的工具,为人们所普遍使用,正如恩格斯所说的,弓箭对于蒙昧时代,正如铁剑对于野蛮时代和火器对于文明时代一样,乃是决定性的武器,弓箭的出现,避免了人和野兽进行面对面的搏斗,提高了远距离杀伤野兽的准确性,弓箭延长了人的手臂和腿,大大增强了我们祖先同自然界斗争的能力。

此外,人们还用石球作成威力很强的"飞球索"来进行狩猎,大大提高了命中率,"飞球索"即在一条藤条或兽筋的两端系上石球,使用时手抓一个石球对准野兽的方向猛力旋转,然后再猛然松开。这样,飞球索在离心力和惯性的作用下会继续旋转,遇到障碍物会自动缠住,这样可以捕捉到逃跑的野兽,飞球索这种世界上最古老的狩猎工具在今天美洲印第安人和非洲的一些原始民族中依然使用着。

半坡人生产活动群雕　　　　猎物的骨骼

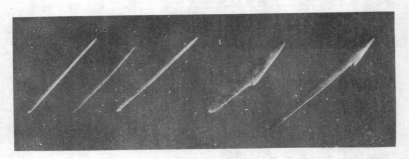

骨针与箭头

狩猎情景想象图

在原始时代，人们为了取得生活资料，并不放弃任何可能采取的手段，为了获取肉食，也可能用斧头、锤头、木棒来攻打野兽，或用陷井、网罗、围猎等方法来捕猎它们。

捕鱼也是半坡人的一项主要经济活动，浐河为人们从事捕鱼生产提供了一个极好的场所，在遗址中发现的捕鱼工具主要有鱼钩、鱼叉和石网坠。

俗话说："姜太公钓鱼，愿者上钩"，传说姜太公钓鱼所用的就是直鱼钩，对于传说的真假我们无法判定，而在半坡遗址中确实发现了没有倒刺的鱼钩、鱼叉，这些早期的直鱼钩、直鱼叉，使用时极不方便，扎上的鱼稍作挣扎就会逃掉，由于人们不断总结经验，最后终于发明了有倒钩和倒刺的鱼钩和鱼叉，它们制作得十分精细，几乎可以和今天的金属鱼钩相媲美，钓鱼的方法也与我们今天的方法相同，估计当时叉鱼法的使用多于钓鱼法。

石网坠是用小而扁平的圆形或椭圆形的河卵石块两侧打击出缺口，使用时系在鱼网底部，来使鱼网沉在河底，鱼网虽未发现，但在发现的彩陶花纹中有索络形鱼纹的纹饰，这从侧面证明了半坡人已经使用网捕法来捕鱼了，当时人们用麻绳结成网，这网即便十分简陋，但也会捕到为数可观的鱼，当然，人们也可能是"竭泽而渔"。

原始的渔猎活动，一个人的力量显得十分单薄，因而集体的作用就充分显示了出来，人们共同协作，集体行动，在渔季，人们甚至会倾村出动，共同体味劳动的艰辛和喜悦。

由于原始的农业生产及其他各种生产活动，还不足以维持人们的物质生活需要，人们仍需从大自然这个仓库中攫取食物加以补充，在遗址中发现的大量螺蛳壳和蚌壳都说明了这一点，此外，人们还采集榛子、栗子、松子和朴树子等果实，采集活动主要由妇女担任,由经验丰富的老年妇女带领儿童在农闲时进行,我们可以想象一下当时人们采集的情景,在聚落附近,人们有的在河边捡拾螺蛳,有的在茫茫苍苍的荒原上采摘野果或挖掘可以食用的块根,有的在挖竹笋或捡拾鸟卵、割取蜂蜜以及可供食用的小昆虫,当然,还有一些令人难以想象的采集对象和获取方式。今天世界上尚有以采集为主的原始民族,如孟加拉湾东部安达曼群岛上的安达曼人就以森林和天然海洋的天然产物为主。

人们为求生存,必须通过各种生产活动来获取生活资料,否则,人类就无法走到今天。

获取了食物,那么如何分配呢?半坡氏族公社时期,土地完全公有,从土地上获取的一切生产物也归部落全体成员共同享有,每个人都有权享有自己的一份,所以,经过大家共同辛苦劳动所得来的东西,是全体成员的公共财富,也归大家所共同拥有。

半坡氏族公社时期对食物实行最严格的共产主义分配,每个人都自觉遵守这一规定,从今天一些民族学资料中可见一斑。印第安人中的一些氏族部落,将捕来的鱼,一起储存,每晚按妇女人数来分配,每人都得到相等的一份。在美洲土人中,财产中最重要的一种东西——食物,决不归个人或家族特别支配。在狩猎中杀死的动物的肉,在不同的部落中,按不同的规则平均分配:火地岛土人遇到荒年时,便跑到海边去寻找食物,如果发现一条搁浅的鲸鱼(这是他们最爱吃的食物),自己再饥饿也不能吃它,而要告诉给全氏族成员,大家一起来,由年长者将鲸肉平均分配;爱斯基摩人那怕只有一块肉,它也是属于大家公有的,而在分配的时候,要考虑到所有的人,特别是病人和没有儿女的寡妇。我们推想半坡人也是采取这种方法来分配食物,参加共食的人,都是平等的。

共食之风的出现,源于生产力低下,生产品极端贫乏。当时,人们往往要忍受可怕的穷困,时时有饥饿、疾病和难以预料的灾难的折磨和牺牲的。在半坡发现的一百五十个成年死者中,平均年龄仅三十多岁,氏族葬地中有三分之一是埋葬小孩的,而且是初生或幼小时就夭折的,这些都说明了当时生活条件的艰苦。只有实行严格的平均分配,才能保证每个成员平等地享受劳动成果,维持大家艰苦贫乏的生活,才有利于生产,否则,就会使一部分社会成员饿死,从而使集体遭到削弱,甚至灭亡。

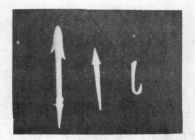

鱼钩和鱼叉

石网坠

半坡人捕鱼情景推想复原图

螺蛳壳

石锛

・15・

半坡人的服饰

　　半坡人在穿衣方面,有了固定的形式,并初步具有了原始审美观念。

　　半坡人衣服的来源有两种,一是兽皮,二是用植物纤维织成的布,人们通过狩猎活动不仅获得肉食,而且获得皮毛,人们用石刀剥取兽皮,之后用陶锉去掉兽皮上的油脂,经过加工的兽皮柔软光滑、美观耐用,是冬季理想的御寒服装。

　　骨梭和陶石纺轮的发现使人们确信了聪明的半坡人已经掌握了纺线织布的技术,他们采用野生植物的纤维,如葛、麻等,用纺轮捻成线,织成布,当时的织布机一种是水平式的,一端固定经线,另一端系在腰际,使用时手持骨梭来回穿引编织。虽然在遗址中没有发现半坡人织出的布,但值得庆幸的是,半坡人在一些陶器的底部留下了十分清晰的麻布印痕,这种麻布粗的类似于今天的麻袋布,细的象帆布。

　　人们在遗址中共发掘出二百八十一枚骨针,制作精美细致,而且在针的尾部已经出现了可供穿线的针眼,这表明当时缝制衣服已相当普遍,至于衣服的式样大概无定型,根据民族学和考古学资料来推测,一种式样大概是连身的,把一块麻布披在身上,腰间系根绳子,这种衣服无上、下衣之分,也无领无袖。另一种式样,"衣"和"裳"可能是分开的,象短衫和短裙,上身主要护胸,无袖,下身主要是护腰和前身,这就是人类最原始的衣裳样式了,衣服的出现不仅用来御寒防暑,还起到了一定的装饰作用。

　　六千七百年前的半坡妇女已经很会装饰自己了,在遗址中发现了与衣服有关的装饰品,种类繁多;从形状上说有环饰、珠饰、坠饰和片状饰;从功用上可分为颈饰,手饰、腰饰还有贴在衣服上的镶嵌饰,几乎从头到脚全身各个部分,都有相适应的装饰品。用作装饰品的材料也相当广泛:有陶的、玉的和石的,也有骨、角、牙和介壳的,这一切充分反映出当时人们已经注意到了美化自己,人们在和半坡遗址同一时期的姜寨遗址发现一个女孩墓。女孩的腰间、颈项及胸前,佩戴着由八千多颗珠子串成的装饰组,真可谓"珠玑盛装"了,而且半坡人已有了束发的习惯,他们将头毛挽结起来用骨笄束住,骨笄,颇似古代妇女头上戴的簪子。

从墓葬中发现的情况来看,装饰品多是妇女佩戴的,如果把这些装饰品佩戴在一个妇女身上,那么在我们面前就显现出一个健美而朴素的原始妇女的形象;在头顶的发束上,插着碧绿的石笄,耳上带着玉耳坠,颈上带着整串的骨珠,胸前佩挂起用兽牙、蚌片和坠子串联起来的镯子,手指上戴着蚌片作的戒指,腰间围排起串珠带子和环饰,走起路来,珠环相碰也许会发出清脆悦耳的声音,她们在制陶、纺织或农业劳动时,这些形声相适调的装饰品大概会引起人们内心的愉快而减轻工作中的疲劳罢。

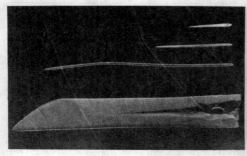

骨梭　骨针　骨刀

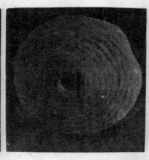

陶制纺轮

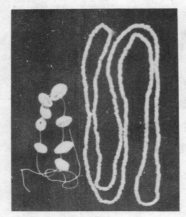

骨珠

陶环

葫芦瓶

细颈瓶

日常生活用具

　　半坡人在日常生活方面所使用的器物是庞杂的,我们推测当时人们已经有了用自然物(如葫芦等)或用木头仿自然物作成的容器,还有用皮革或麻布制成的袋囊以及用竹藤之类编成的筐篮,这些器物都容易腐朽,随着时间的推移,它们早已消失于灰烬垃圾之中,给我们留到现在的只是大量的式样繁复的陶器。

　　说到陶器,必然要谈谈陶器是如何发明出来的。起先,人类在编织或木制的容器外部涂上泥巴放在火上烧烤食物,涂泥的目的,在于使容器耐火,结果发现篮子被火烧掉了,成型的泥土也可以起到耐火的作用;于是从这个偶然的发现中发明了陶器,我国流传着关于宁封制陶的古老传说正是对陶器发明的生动描述:宁封偶然从火烧野兽的现象中得到启发,领悟到火烧的泥土十分坚硬,于是懂得了作陶器的原理,从而作了黄帝的陶正,陶器的出现,具有划时代的意义,而制陶术则是人类对于化学变化的最早利用,对于科学的发端,有着重大的意义。

　　半坡人制陶的技术水平相当高,他们作出的器物也很精美,但由于生产力水平的限制,仍保留在手制阶段。

　　手制主要用两种方法:一种是泥条盘筑法,一种是捏塑法,泥条盘筑法又可以分为两种作法:一种是旋筑法,这种方法是用细的泥条盘旋而成,作出的器物形小壁薄,第二种是叠筑法,是将泥条一圈一圈的加上去,或一片一片地叠筑起来。

　　制作陶器时,一般是先作器底,大的器底是用泥条盘筑的,小的多用泥片捏成,粗陶制的瓮罐之类的器物底部往往加垫一圈泥条,使之坚固。在底部作成后,一般在接底部的边沿依次加添泥条作成壁腹,器物腹部的作法比较复杂,在用泥条盘筑法的同时,外表用手按捏,内部用陶具垫压,而这些压垫工具形如蘑菇,它有一个直径约六厘米左右的圆形球面的头部,后面加一个握手的把柄,这种工具的大小视所制器物体形的大小和质地的粗细而异。

制造比较大型的器物,尤其是制造这些器物的腹部时,偶而也使用模制,模制大概是外面用模子加以规范,里面用泥条或泥条盘筑,口部制作,大多是作好后加接上去的,也有些在直口上用戴帽子的方法,加在顶部,然后向外或向内捏塑。

器物的雏形作成后,还要作一系列的修饰和附加工作,例如大型的瓮缸之类器物,作成之后,底部内外都要加垫泥条。器物的腹部则加些凸饰,这些都是在制作时考虑到巩固器壁和实用性而作的,不是纯粹为了装饰。

修饰器物使之美观也是制陶过程的一个主要工序。这项工作大概是用竹质或木质的工具如刀、匕之类,先将陶坯切削,使器物的造型更加优美。

制作陶器的最后一个工序,是将陶坯放到陶窑里去烧,在半坡遗址的东面,就是半坡人的陶窑区,在这里发现了六座保留下来比较完好的陶窑,从发现的陶窑的形状大小来推测,当时烧窑的规模并不大,在一个窑里,一般陶坯每次只能放四、五个,小的可放二、三十个,大的只能放一、两个。

从半坡遗址中出土的六座陶窑可以说是中国最古老的陶窑,分横穴窑和竖穴窑两种形式,每座陶窑均由火膛、火道、窑箅和窑室几部分组成,横穴窑是半坡人早期使用的陶窑,其形状为:最下面是一个火膛,呈长而倾斜的筒状,长约两米左右;最上面是窑室,在火膛倾斜方向的后方,直径一米左右,圆穹状;火膛与窑室之间是放置陶坯的窑箅,窑箅中心及两侧有三条大火道,窑箅周围有一圈等距离的十二、三个圆形或弓形的火眼,这些火眼距火膛近的较小,距火膛远的则较大,以调节窑内温度,使陶坯受热均匀。竖穴窑是半坡后期出现的,构造较横穴窑先进,其最大的特点是火膛在窑室的垂直下方,火膛通窑室的距离近,圆形袋状;窑箅中间有两个粗而圆的洞作为火道,这种窑比横穴窑体积略大。

烧制陶器则以木柴为燃料,经鉴定当时窑内温度可达800—1000℃左右,烧制出的彩陶器颜色大多美而纯正。

半坡的陶窑虽然形制粗陋、结构简单,但它却完整而合理,可以说是先民聪明才智和探索精神的杰出体现,在当时烧制出了满足人们各种生活需要的陶器,立下了汗马功劳,亦为后来中国以瓷国著称于世奠定了坚实的基础。

半坡的陶器从质料上又可分为夹砂陶和细泥陶两大类。夹砂陶是在陶土中掺些粗砂粒,作出的陶器不很严密,但耐火性强,遇热不易破裂,具有今天使用的砂锅的性能,可以承受热胀冷缩的自然变化,主要是半坡人用以烧煮食物的炊具。

而细泥陶制作的陶器外表光滑美观、质地坚硬,主要用于盛水、饮食方面。

半坡人制作出的陶器的种类是相当丰富的,今天我们日常生活上用的那几种基本类型的器物,那时都有,就用途上讲,可分为饮食器、炊煮器、水器和储藏器等。

饮食用的器物主要有陶碗、陶钵、陶盆、陶盂等种,还有类似于今天高脚酒杯的陶豆,不同形状的器物都服务于不同的生活需要,这式样繁多的饮食器向我们展示了远古人类丰富的生活内涵。

粗砂陶炊具主要有陶甑,陶甑是半坡人用来蒸食物(主要是小米)的,其形状如盆、钵、碗类,它的底部有方形或圆形的规则小孔,与陶盖、陶罐配套使用,在加工食物时,将陶甑配装在盛有水的陶罐上,盖上陶盖,然后在陶罐底部烧火加热,当水沸腾时,蒸汽便通过小孔进入陶甑,使陶甑中的食物变熟,这就是延续至今的我国北方每户必备的蒸笼和蒸锅的雏形,也可以说它是聪明的半坡人在六千七百年以前对蒸汽原理的最早应用。

水器多为细泥陶制,主要有尖底瓶、葫芦瓶、细颈壶和带流器等。

尖底瓶,是半坡人主要的运水工具,它口小、短颈、鼓腹、尖底、两侧有耳,外形有点象橄榄,半坡人把尖底瓶做为盛水器皿是有其科学道理的。尖底瓶通体呈流线型,运水时,因口小,即使颠簸的厉害,也不致使水洒出,而鼓腹,增加了容水量,尖底则可以分散水对于瓶底的压力,两侧有耳,系上绳后,背负肩挎皆宜,男女老少均可使用,更为奇妙的是,把它放入水中,它会自动倾倒,灌满水后,又会自动立起,经鉴定,尖底瓶已基本符合了物理学上的重心原理。

半坡人仿照野生葫芦形状作出来的葫芦瓶,既美观,又实用,狩猎时携带十分方便,堪与今日的行军水壶相媲美。

早期的葫芦瓶是完全模仿了野生葫芦的形状,后来,由于实用和美观的要求,逐渐脱离了葫芦的原型,改变了器物单一的向外凸弧的外形,细颈壶就是将葫芦瓶变形之后产生的另一种水器,它头部外鼓而细颈内束,上腹圆凸而下腹曲收,呈反复的有节奏的对比,而又统一于弧形的造型之中,使器物有着生动的曲线变化,十分优美动人。

当人们看到带流器时往往会联想到我们今天使用的茶壶,

带流器,有一个凸出的部分称作流,相当于茶壶嘴,它可以使液体集中起来倒入口比较小的容器中。

　　储藏器主要有大型的陶瓮、陶缸,是用来装粮食和水的,还发现了一个半坡晚期的大尖底瓶,它很可能是用来储水,大尖底瓶有着奇特的外形,仔细观察如同一位妇女的形体,可能是一位妇女,在制作时在陶器中溶入了自己的形象,那流畅的线条,优雅的造型令人赏心悦目,这说明了原始人已具备了初步的审美意识。

　　大型的陶缸和陶瓮,体积大,四壁均匀,结实耐用,说明当时人们在制陶技术上已经达到了一定的水平,同时,又说明了已经有一些人专门从事制陶生产,从而积累了丰富的经验,掌握了熟练的技能,这就为以后手工业从农业中分离出来打下了基石。

陶碗　　　　　　　　　　陶罐

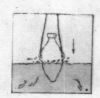

尖底瓶重心原理示意图

陶罐

陶豆

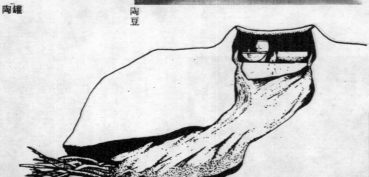

陶窑

刻划符号

　　文字的发明，也是有其发生、发展的过程，最初人类有可能采用物件作符号来记事，或者是"结绳记事、契木为文。"世界上有许多原始部落都保留有结绳记事、契木为文的残余。大洋洲各岛的土著人，彼此以绳子打结来传达消息，北美洲印第安人则用系着各种贝壳的带子来记事，我国少数民族在历史上，甚至在解放前夕还用结绳记事的方法，那么六千多年前的半坡人有没有文字呢？

　　其实，在半坡也有类似于文字的刻划符号，半坡人留给后人最扑朔迷离的疑问就是那些刻在陶钵外口缘的黑宽带或黑色倒三角内的刻划符号，共计一百一十三个标本，二十二种，这些符号笔划大多均匀流畅，相当规整，部分笔划简单，部分笔划已相当复杂，从刻划符号的形状上看，与后来出现的甲骨文十分相像，而且，除半坡遗址外，另外发现刻划符号的其它仰韶文化的九个遗址都位于关中地区，这与甲骨文的发现地是吻合的，这说明萌芽于仰韶文化彩陶上的刻划符号，很有可能是甲骨文的前身，是中华文字的渊源之一。

　　再者，甲骨文，文法灵活多变，词汇丰富，所反映的社会内容已相当广泛，涉及政治、军事、文化、农业、气象、宗教、信仰、风俗习惯等，可以想象，没有几百到上千年循序渐进的发展决不可能达到如此的高度。

　　半坡人的刻划符号，已经初步具有了记事和表意的功能，也可能当时人们还在木质器物上书写或刻划有更多的符号，只是由于木质器物易腐烂而无法保存下来，由于刻划符号数量的限制,要想证明这些刻划符号是何种文字或发何种音是十分困难的,有待于进一步的研究。

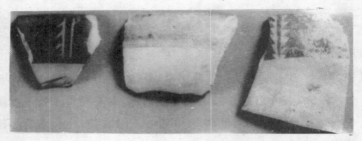

陶器刻纹

划纹符号

陶碗上的刻纹

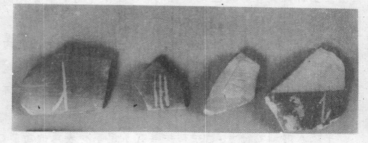

半坡陶器上的刻纹

半坡的彩陶器及陶塑

凡到过半坡的人都会被那色彩雅致、独具魅力的彩陶器所吸引,半坡的彩陶器上有漂亮的彩绘纹饰,纹饰绚丽多彩,笔触均匀流畅,令人叹为观止,那么当时的画家是用什么作画的呢?

考古工作者在发掘距半坡村落遗址不远的姜寨遗址时,在仰韶文化早期地层中发现了一位六千年前的画家的墓葬,在画家的身旁发现了一套画具,这是迄今为止我国发现的最早的画具,这套画具包括一方带盖石砚,一根石研棒和一件陶水杯,还有几块红色颜料,经过鉴定,红色颜料成份为三氧化二铁,估计当时已有画笔,因年代太久已腐朽不存,画具的发现,揭开了半坡人绘画之谜,目前,这套远古画具已展示在半坡博物馆内。

半坡彩陶以其简洁的艺术形象和寓意深刻的图案,反映出半坡氏族人们丰富多彩的精神世界。

半坡彩陶的出现标志着黄河中下游地区的彩陶艺术进入了迅猛发展的阶段,在制作技术、器物造型、图案艺术等方面都有了突出的进步。半坡仰韶文化的彩陶是继承老官台文化彩陶发展起来的。老官台文化的制陶工艺比较原始,彩陶器表粗糙,色彩粗浊,灰暗,并易脱落,彩陶的彩绘效果很差,而半坡彩陶有着明净的质地,陶土不含砂粒且有韧性;由于烧制火候较高,器表又打磨得很光滑,使陶器显得精美细润;彩绘颜色的种类也增多了,除红、白两色外,大量地使用黑彩。黑彩以二氧化锰为着色剂,但经过研细加工,色泽较鲜明。以深色的彩纹画在洁净光润的细泥红陶上,显得清新醒目,具有爽朗动人的风采。

量体裁衣,半坡人也懂得根据不同的器形来装饰不同格式的图案,图案与器形相得益障,配置和谐,口沿在器形最上方的部位,也是器物最宽的地方,所以选择了显眼的口沿外圈来装饰图案花纹,并且常常以几何形纹组成二方连续图案,像精致的彩带围在口边,彩陶的器形大多是中型的圆卷唇折腹盆,上腹有较宽的装饰面可以用来绘制花纹,可以表现内容较复杂的图案。在这类盆的上腹常绘着写实的鱼纹或变体鱼纹,以鱼的各种纹样连续地或间隔地作一圈排列,犹如鱼在循环不已地游动,半坡彩陶不仅根据器形的凹凸和宽窄来决定图案的布局,还注意到当时人们在生活中看陶器时常取的视线角度,将图案花纹饰于陶器的一目了然的位置上。像盆内敞开的腹壁、陶器鼓凸的上部这些人们视力常及的部位,多以人面、鱼、鹿、网纹等单独纹样分成等距的四个单元排成一圈,饰于其上,而在人们视线不常及的陶器下部和凹处则不绘花纹。像细颈壶这类小型的彩陶,人们可以在使用时随意地升降其安放的位置,半坡陶工在设计这类彩陶的图案布局时,就考虑到从不同角度去看彩陶所产生的不同感觉,如折腹细颈彩陶壶的上腹,在平视时的平面形象近于三角形,而俯视时则会发现彩陶壶变成了盛开的花朵,壶口就成了它的花蕊部分。由于半坡彩陶其装饰花纹的组合、黑白、大小、繁简均合于美的韵律,形成了协调的节奏感,使人们看了感到轻松舒畅,美感和实用性达到了十分和谐完美的程度,反映了人们审美观念的提高。

半坡彩陶上的图案,式样繁多,种类丰富,几何形的图案纹样造型规整、结构缜密,有强烈的装饰性,而以仿生物的纹样组成的图案,造型奇特,寓意深奥,具有象征意味和神秘色彩。

半坡彩陶的几何形图案花纹,最早源于编织物的几何形花纹,经过长期的发展,逐渐脱离了编织物的原始骨式,演绎出许多新的几何纹样和图案格式,不再是写实地模拟编织物,只是示意地表示出编织物的形象。

彩陶上源自编织物的几何形纹样,反映了当时人们在早期的陶器生产中的信念:他们认为只有将陶器做成原来做为器皿的编织物的形状和纹样,才能具有原器皿的功能,但是事实上饰于陶器上的这种模拟纹样已不再具有编织物的肌理纹样在物质生产中的功能,已不是物质生产的组成部分,这时的几何形花纹组成的图案,已经纯粹是人们审美观念的艺术生产了。

仿生性纹饰有鱼纹、鹿纹和人面形纹等,其中又以鱼纹的数量为最多,贯穿于半坡仰韶文化的始终,为半坡彩陶中具有代表性的花纹。

半坡彩陶的鱼纹发展源远流长,呈现出由写实模拟的自然形纹演变为写意的几何形纹样的完整系列。

早期的彩陶上的鱼纹有着简练单纯的艺术风格,大部分是形象写实的单独纹样,鱼往往呈现出一种悠然于水、大口食食的稚态,鱼的形体概括、造型明确,直观的形象感很强,外廓呈前倾的三角形,寥寥几笔,传神地刻划出鱼向前游动的姿态,由于当时的人们还没有掌握用透视的法则去观察事物,所以,早期的鱼纹只是将鱼的形象平舒地展开,选用了表现力强的正侧面角度,完整无缺地画出鱼的头(有的还画出须、牙等细部)鳃、身、鳍、尾各个部分。虽然基本上还是依照鱼的自然形作写实的描绘,但经过选形、选视点、选角度的艺术处理,简单而整体地表现出鱼的形象,在单纯质朴的造型中流露出天真稚拙的情趣,给人以亲切自然的感觉。

到了后期,随着氏族社会的不断发展,鱼纹图案被赋予了更新的含意,即用象征的手法来表示复杂的内涵,鱼纹被进行了夸张变形的艺术处理，已经不再全面、如实地描绘整条鱼，只是用鱼的具有特征的某一部分（如：头、身子和尾）来表现鱼，由此发展到最后的鱼是以三角形表示鱼头，中间点上一个小点表示鱼的眼睛。这时彩陶上的鱼纹已不是自然界中真实而具体的鱼，而是将鱼的具有特征的某一部分浓缩凝炼成标志性的纹样，示意地表现了理念中的概念化的鱼。这充分体现了半坡绘画艺术由写实到写意、由具体到抽象的演变过程。

绘有鹿纹的陶器出土的并不多，在发现的一个鹿纹盆的内壁上绘有四只小鹿，它们警惕地伫立注目，如临大敌，随时准备应付可能将至的灭顶之灾，鹿的形象被勾勒得维妙维肖、栩栩如生，具有中国画的传统写实风格，表现出原始艺术家敏锐而质朴的观察能力和充沛的、无拘无束的娴熟的艺术技巧。

尽管半坡人以农业生产为主，但是狩猎和捕鱼在半坡人的生活中仍占有很重要的地位，无论是鱼纹盆、鹿纹盆还是网纹盆，都是和当时人们的生活有关，是渔猎活动的反映，到了后期，随着农业生产的发展，人们能够有规律地自己生产产品，因而减少了对自然界的依赖，逐渐加强了社会意识，因而，在半坡彩陶图案中出现了人面衔鱼、鱼头寓有人面等奇特的图案花纹。

人面鱼纹彩陶盆，图案以人头和鱼身组成，滚圆的头形，戴着尖顶的饰物；细长的弯眉，眯合成一线的双眼；倒置的"丁"字形鼻子，大嘴作对顶的三角形，连接耳部还各有一条小鱼，整个画面将人头和鱼身巧妙地结合在一起，夸张得恰到好处，十分有趣。半坡人不厌其烦地将鱼的纹样绘制在陶器上，又使人与鱼相结合而成人面鱼纹，人鱼形象的合二为一，这在自然界中是不存在的，那么，我们又该如何理解这种奇特纹样的含义呢？看来，半坡人喜欢鱼崇拜鱼，故鱼很可能成了半坡氏族的图腾，即认为它们的氏族起源于鱼，我国古籍上就有人鱼互变的神话。《山海经》中就记载着颛顼死后复苏，化身为鱼的故事。这就包含着以鱼为祖先，死则返祖复原的图腾崇拜观念。

在人类的童年时代，无法对自身的起源作出正确的解答，而大自然所给予人类的轻则是狂风暴雨、电闪雷鸣；重则是山洪暴发，地震海啸，这些既使人们恐惧，又使他们感到无法解释，不得不祈求山、水、植物等神灵，以得到它们的庇护，因而在氏族形成过程中，氏族往往以猛兽或有特殊功能的动物为保护神，人们将某种植物或动物奉作自己的血亲祖先加以崇拜，由此产生了图腾崇拜，在半坡时期，氏族公社制已很繁盛，与这种社会制度相联系的图腾崇拜现象也相当发达。而图腾的图象，往往表现在人们日常生活及艺术活动的各方面，半坡彩陶所绘的鱼纹、鹿纹，大概就是氏族图腾的徽号，而视那人头鱼身的图象为氏族的图腾徽号就显得更加合理了，至今我国一些少数民族中依然残存着动物崇拜的遗迹。例如：白族还沿袭着以鱼和海螺为殉葬品的习俗，这一习俗，无疑源于动物崇拜，白族妇女一直盛行以鱼尾帽为头饰，这亦源于对鱼崇拜的祭祀活动。而在远古时代氏族多以动物或生物命名，例如有蛴氏、神农氏（神龙氏），有熊氏等，汉族中马、牛、李、梅、林、龙等姓氏，就是图腾名称的遗迹。而台湾高山族以蛇或陶器为图腾，瑶族和畲族以犬为图腾、鄂伦春族以熊为图腾等等，都是图腾制的遗俗。

总之，半坡人很可能认为他们的祖先是鱼，或者是人格化了的人头鱼身的动物。

半坡彩陶器那鲜明的色彩、典雅的风格使世人为之惊叹，具有永不凋谢的艺术魅力，堪称我国远古艺术宝库中一朵瑰丽的奇葩。

半坡人除了制作出色彩绚丽的几何形图案,加工小巧玲珑的各类装饰品,而且制作出了古朴、稚拙的陶塑品,这些陶塑以造型优美、神态逼真而堪称原始艺术中的珍品。

陶塑内容,多取材于人类生活中最熟悉的动物。另外还有表现人类本身的人面陶塑。半坡的鸟形陶塑、兽形陶塑均为器盖把守,鸟形陶塑,轮廓清晰,头颈俱全,颇似鸽子,眼睛用锥刺来表示,兽形陶塑,头似兽类,尾似鸟类,作正视伫立状,耳眼均用锥刺表现,口部则划一道浅横线示之,面孔似狗又似羊,仔细观来,妙趣横生。

人头形陶塑用泥块捏塑而成,扁头方脸,大耳高鼻,眼深凹,耳根上还有耳孔,耳目口鼻均用泥片附加粘合而成。陶塑的用途似为插在某种东西上的附饰或儿童的玩具,体现出远古人类对自身的形态、面貌、力量的认识和艺术的再现能力。

半坡的陶塑品告诉我们远古时代的艺术总是首先从实用出发,然后才考虑其审美价值的,作为器盖钮的陶塑也许告诉人们这时的审美意识已进入实用与观赏并存的时期。

在半坡有两只陶哨特别惹人注意,这两只陶哨又称陶埙被称作"魔笛",它是目前我国发现的最古老的吹奏乐器之一,它形状奇特,今天还可以吹响两个以上的音节,它的音程、音色和音调与秦腔音乐所表现出的风格、特点十分相似,因此,我们可以认为半坡陶埙是秦声的最早见证。当然,在六千七百年以前,陶哨也可能是作为人们的联络工具使用的。

陶埙

刻纹陶瓶

陶鸟首

彩陶

陶兽

半坡人的村落布局及房屋建筑

　　大家都知道,"衣、食、住"是人们生活中必不可少的三要素,前面已谈到半坡人的"衣"、"食"及有关种种,现在来谈谈半坡人的"住",具体地讲,就是半坡遗址,半坡遗址比较完整地保留了六千七百多年以前人们聚居的村落和住房等建筑遗址,是一座有规划的典型的母系氏族公社的村落遗址。

　　半坡遗址可以说是目前所发现的仰韶文化聚落遗址中最大的,总面积为五万平方米,包括居住区、陶窑区和墓葬区三个部分,居住区约为三万平方米,现已发掘了北部约五分之一的面积,居住区周围还设有宽深各约五到六米的围沟围护,沟北为公墓区,沟东为陶窑生产区。居住、墓葬、制陶用地的区分,反映出半坡人已具有了规划的观念。当人们开始最初的定居生活时,住房、陶窑甚至墓葬可能都是混杂在一起的,随着社会发展,人们根据需要为便于制陶生产而将陶窑集中于一区,并将死者埋葬到居住区以外的地方,因之萌发了原始的规划思想。将居住区与墓葬区隔离的划分方法也是符合卫生条件的一个重大进步。

　　通过对居住区的发掘和清理,共得房屋遗迹四十六座,储存东西的地窖二百多个,饲养家畜的圈栏两座,埋葬小孩的瓮棺七十三座,围绕村庄的大沟一条,生产工具和生活用具一万多件,从已发掘的居住区可以看出,当时村庄的布局已经相当的井然有序了,位于居住区中心的,是一个面积为一百六十平方米的大房子,村庄里其它小房屋的门都向着它开,构成了一个向心状布局,从形式上反映出这座大房屋的重要性。

　　那么,这座大房屋的作用究竟是什么呢?根据民族学的资料推测，它首先是供老人和儿童居住的地方，其次是举行宗教礼仪、祭祀活动的场所，如当少年成年后便在这里举行一种成丁礼（进入成年的标志），仪式结束后，此人就从大房屋中搬出组成一个对偶家庭。因此可以说，大房屋是氏族成员成长的摇篮。同时，人们在这里举行氏族议事会，讨论劳动产品的分配、选举氏族首领等等，从某种意义上说，这座房屋是我们今天大会堂的雏形。

所有小房子的门都朝向大房子，这种住房的环形布置，使得约有半数住房的日照、通风条件较差，这种优先保证总体的布置，首先是以共产制为基础的集体生活所决定的，因此，在建筑群的面貌上，明显地体现着团结向心的公社组织原则，它说明氏族成员被血缘纽带连接在一起，并依赖氏族而生存着。

半坡的小房屋面积都为二十平方米左右，从形式上分为圆形和方形两种。从结构上则分为半地穴室和地面上建筑两种形式。

圆形房屋和方形房屋在细部构造上略有不同，但其基本特征是相同的，大多是采用半地穴式的建筑形式，每个房子里面，中心有一个火塘（灶坑），可以用来取暖照明和烧烤食物，在火塘和门道之间，是一个方形的门坎，可以防止雨水倒灌，屋内地面和墙壁，都是用草泥土涂抹得相当光滑平整，房屋的方位相同，相互之间有一定的距离（1—3 米），位置排列的比较规则。

方形房屋以半地穴室为主，少数是从平地建筑起来的。从地面向下挖一个方形土坑的半地穴式房屋，它有坑壁即墙壁，再在其上覆以四面坡的草棚，那么为什么要将房屋建成半地穴室的样子呢？这主要是当时人们刚刚从洞穴生活中发展到平原，还不会打墙盖房，但是从地面向下挖一个方形土坑，以坑壁为墙壁，这样就容易得多了，但是由于房子伸入地下，所以比较阴暗潮湿,房屋内地面平整。晚期方形房子作高低不同的两个部分,高的部分在屋子的左半侧,低的在右半侧,各约占房屋面积的一半,高的部分可能是人们睡觉的土炕,低的部分大概是放置用具和食物的,或者是男女分别卧息的界限,可见,到了半坡晚期屋室内已形成了合理的布局。

方形房屋中从平地上建筑起来的很少,但有一座房子特别典型,可以说是当时最先进的建筑,而且,在建筑技术上也比其它房子复杂。支撑房屋的柱子已经开始分工。这座房屋由十二根大木柱所支撑,柱子插入地内达半米之深,列为整齐的三排,每排四根,这样,由两旁向中间一行搭设柱子就会形成一个人字形两面坡的房子,而且中间的四根柱子大致在一条线上,说明脊檩已达两山,即四柱等高,顶部密排板椽或其它材料,最后内外厚抹草泥。它标志中间以间架为单位的"墙倒房不塌"的古典木构框架体系已趋形成,这座房子复原起来的人字形两面坡屋顶的房子。直立的墙体、倾斜的屋盖,奠定了后世建筑的基本体形。我国民族建筑中的传统风格就是从这里开始的。

中国传统的"一明两暗"或"前堂后室"的建筑风格可以从半坡的建筑特征里追根溯源。半坡早期房屋从防水出发所设的门道雨棚,可以减少雨雪对内部空间的袭击及弥补居寝暴露的缺陷,从而使内部空间较为隐蔽和安全,而门道雨棚,又恰似"堂"的雏形,再向屋内发展,形成了后世的明间,隔墙左右形成两个次间,正是"一明两暗"的形式,如若横向来看,又将隔室与室内分成前后两个部分,形成"前堂后室"的格局,古代阶级社会中的"前朝后寝"的宫室正是源于半坡的这种"前堂后室"。

圆形房子也有两种不同的样式,一种是用木架建筑起来的,另一种是半地穴室的,复原起来,前者象一个蒙古包,后者却象一个截尖的圆锥体,这种房子全是用粗的木椽、木柱和大量的粘土混合建筑起来的。

半坡的房屋均采用的是木骨涂泥的构筑方法,即在地上挖出小洞,将木柱插入,在柱子内外涂以草泥使其成为墙壁。半坡人留给了我们四百多个柱洞遗迹。柱洞的制法是先将地面挖一个呈圆形的小坑,底部垫一层粘土夯实。柱子埋入后,四周铺上石块和破陶片,再铺泥土砸实,有的则在柱子四周堆起厚约十几公分的土堆。这样就可以将柱子的负荷重量分散在较大的面积上。它可以说是我国建筑史上最早的柱础,它比把木柱直接埋入地下要坚固得多,对柱础的加工,是半坡人建筑技术发展的标志之一。

半坡人还发明了烧烤防潮工艺。由于半穴居的下部空间是挖掘自然土地构成,穴底和四壁都保持着黄土的自然结构,由于毛细现象,使得地面潮湿,长期居住,轻则患湿气疥癣,重则引起关节炎,风湿性心脏病等症,《墨子》中就有"下润湿伤民"的记述,惨痛的生活经验迫使人们开始探求防潮的方法,最早人们主要是铺垫较厚的茅草、皮毛之类防潮,到了半坡时期,已相当进步,人们在地面铺以草泥土,并且用火反复烧烤,而在半坡中期还出现了以木材之类作为防潮层的作法。

在日照方位的选择上,半坡时期的居住建筑呈西南向的规律性,这一方位显然是由日照决定的,建筑方位尽管与聚落布局有关,但在保证总体关系的条件下,仍以日照为选定方位的准则,半坡已发掘的位于广场北部的四十余座建筑遗址,本应南向,然而大部分出入口却偏向西南。半坡建筑有门无窗,出入口兼备交通、采光、日照、通风诸功能,原始居民不是由科学计算,而是通过生活经验和营造实践,得出朝向西南和将入口提高到适应日照要求高度的合理结论,这不知经历了几多世代的反复探索。

半坡人在彩陶艺术上所表现出的审美能力和创作水平使我们相信他们在用粘土塑造出来的建筑造型上,也是会有形、色的装饰处理的,人们曾在西安附近姜寨遗址和宝鸡北首岭遗址中发现了门窗口的塑型图案浮雕残迹,而《西安半坡》(半坡遗址发掘报告)中还发表了一个列入建筑残件的高浮雕或圆浮雕泥塑残块似为动物的形象,如报告无误,就可以证明仰韶文化建筑装饰已有相当的发展了,对门窗之类的重点处理,手法经济,效果显著,堪称六千年前劳动先民的杰出创造。

在居住区内,人们还发现了半坡人使用过的公共地窖的遗迹,共二百多个,全部分布在屋外的空地上,是集体储存生产资料和生活资料的公共仓库,这显然是氏族公有制的一种体现。地窖分早、晚两期,早期地窖容积小、数量少,形式多样;晚期地窖则容积大、数量多,形式固定——一般是口小底大的圆形袋状窖穴,这一发展趋势,体现了随着生产的发展而出现的公共积累的增加。这些地窖制作得都非常讲究,内壁涂以草泥土并用火烧烤,使其光滑平整,坚硬干燥,经过这样的处理,使它成为储存农作物的理想场所。

另外,我们还可以看到这样一条小沟,从表面来看,这条小沟的宽和深均为一点八米,分东西两段,互不相通,而且内沟没有发现流水的痕迹,可见其作用不在排水,另外,从小沟的走向来看,它一直穿过居住区的中心,将村庄分为两个部分。由此推测,它的作用可能在借以区分不同的氏族或同一氏族中不同的家族及集团,类似于现在的界墙。而且,小沟只存在于早期,到了晚期,它逐渐被生活垃圾所充塞,小沟的兴衰之变,也许暗示着氏族组织的荣枯变化吧！

　　那么，在六千七百年前半坡人所处的野蛮时代，人们是否曾有过抵御外来侵扰的防卫设施呢？回答是肯定的，六千多年以前的氏族村落中不但有，而且规模宏大，半坡遗址居住区周围，环绕有一条全长三百米、宽六到八米，深五到六米的大围沟，沟的底部宽四米，并发现有木柱的痕迹，可能在围沟底部和两旁曾设有防御之类的障碍物。大围沟的作用主要有两个，其一，可用来防水、排水，其二可以避免野兽侵扰，防止各部落之间氏族成员因血亲复仇而发生的冲突，所以，大围沟被视为六千年前的"护城河"。

　　在原始公社时期，人类要生存，就要与大自然作斗争，大围沟便是这一斗争的产物。大围沟使我们看到了祖先的勤劳和勇敢，它的总出土量为一万一千立方米，如用三吨位的卡车，可装载三千六百六十六辆，如此艰巨的工程，我们很难想象它竟完成于六千年前的石器时代，从中可以看到半坡先民集体协作的伟大创造力。

　　　　　圆形屋复原图　　长方形屋复原图

方形屋复原图

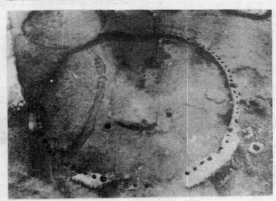

上图为方形屋残基

下图为圆形屋残基

半坡氏族的墓葬习俗及信仰和婚姻形态

　　半坡的埋葬习俗使我们看到当时人们的思想意识和精神活动，半坡先民可以说是原始宗教的狂热信奉者。他们不仅虔诚地崇拜作为氏族标志的图腾和从事农业祭祀等方面的宗教活动，而且，在丧葬方面也十分讲究，有成套严格的、纷繁复杂的丧葬习俗，半坡遗址墓地死者的埋葬形式之多，出土墓葬之完整在同时期遗址墓地当中可以说是屈指可数的。

儿童的葬俗

　　半坡人对小孩和成人的葬法是不同的，成人死后以各种方式埋葬于公共墓地，而不幸夭折的小孩却用瓮棺葬在居住区内房屋的附近，最多的葬具是用一个粗陶瓮或大罐盛装尸体，上面盖一个陶钵或陶盆，比较大的小孩，则用两个大瓮对起来埋葬。

　　成人和儿童分开埋葬的习俗，在考古学和民族学资料中，都可以找到类同的事例，如：安达曼岛上的土著居民大人死后埋在村子外面，却把小孩埋在房子下面；佤族埋人时，大人在公共墓地中按姓氏分开，小孩则用竹席捆起，葬在自己房子附近，也不放随葬品，广东省连南瑶族自治县南岗等地的瑶族同胞，凡本家族的成年人死后都须葬入家族墓地当中，以表示相互间的血肉感情。但是，儿童死后却不得葬入，按当地习惯，未满月的婴儿死亡，只能埋葬在自家房屋内父母亲的床下，他们认为婴儿年幼，尚需父母照应，埋在野外，大人不放心。又如，贵州省荔波县瑶山公社的白裤瑶早先是行岩洞葬，解放前夕已改行土葬，但是，按习惯凡十岁以下的孩子死亡后一般不殓入棺,并且不得葬入祖墓之内,否则为不吉。夭亡婴儿则须葬在村寨附近的低凹之处,不得与成年人葬在一起。

将成年人与儿童分开埋葬的习俗的产生与一个人的成年与否也有一定的关系,解放前在云南纳西族有此习俗,男孩和女孩长到十三岁时要分别举行穿裤子礼和穿裙子礼,它实际上是一个人成年的标志,经此仪式之后,男女方可进入各种社交场合,从此之后,他们便也取得了家庭正式成员的资格,只有举行过此种仪式的成年男女,在他们死亡之后才能葬入本"斯日"(即家族)的公共墓地,另外,过去云南布朗族的习俗,年满十五岁的男女青年在进入社交前须经一种特殊仪式,由成丁年龄的男青年和成丁年龄的女青年用一种树木燃烧后的黑烟互相染齿,这实际上也是一种成丁仪式,从此他们便开始进入自己崭新的生活历程,进行谈情说爱之类的活动。

上述事实告诉我们,半坡的儿童瓮棺葬首先充分体现出母亲对孩子的体贴和爱护,因死者年幼,母亲不忍心自己的骨肉被野兽伤害,埋在屋子附近便于经常照看,正如郭沫若先生在诗中所写的:"半坡小儿冢、瓮棺盛尸骸,瓮棺有圆孔、气可通内外。墓集居址旁,仿佛尤在怀;大人则无棺,纵横陈荒隈。可知爱子心,万劫永不灰"。其次,由于举行过成丁礼的人才能算作本氏族的正式成员,生时既是本氏族或本家族的人,那么,死亡后到另一个世界也应当是本氏族或本家族的鬼,他们也应当同死去的祖宗聚集一堂共同生活,理应埋入公共墓地。反之,未举行过成丁礼的儿童,因其尚未成年,在生之时不算是本氏族或本家族的正式成员,死亡之后也勿须葬入氏族的公共墓地,这正是半坡人将成年人和儿童分开埋葬的含义。

值得注意的是,绝大多数作为瓮棺盖子的陶盆或陶缸底部中间都有一个人工凿制成或敲击而成的小孔。半坡人人为制作这样的小孔,其意义何在呢?

其实,在瓮棺上有意钻凿小孔的现象并非半坡独有,直到解放前在我国一些民族地区还存在着类似现象,比如,四川冕宁县和爱公社庙顶等地的藏族主要是行火葬,将死者火化后把骨灰装入陶罐再埋入土中,陶罐底部都作有一小孔,用意是"让灵魂出而归西"。在贵州省荔波县瑶山公社的白裤瑶中还存在着一种更为奇特的现象,即在死者坟头插一根竹竿,竹竿的每一节都应打通,插入坟内的一端应对着死者的嘴部位置,当地人称这根竹竿为"归宗竹",意即死者的灵魂通过这根竹竿就能同死去的祖先团聚,在我国的另一些民族地区,虽不是在葬具上打孔,但却要在坟墓上打洞或筑门,有的在坟顶部的左侧掘一小洞,以便尔后举行墓祭活动时由此投放祭品,供死者食用。从以上这些事例,我们可以得出一个合乎逻辑的看法,半坡小孩瓮棺上钻凿的孔洞应为灵魂出入的通道,可见,当时人们的思想意识中不仅存在着灵魂观念,而且,这种观念已相当复杂和系统了。

除了瓮棺外,在遗址中发现的一个女孩墓十分特殊,墓主是一个三、四岁的小女孩,以木椁为葬具,仰身直肢,随葬品有陶器六件,骨珠六十九颗,粮食一钵,玉石耳坠一枚,石球三颗,而在姜寨遗址,表现得更为显著,死者是一个十六、七岁的少女,**随葬品有二十三件之多**;计有玩具的石珠十二粒,玉耳坠两个,石刀一个,陶钵、陶罐和尖底瓶各一件,特别罕见的是用八千五百六十三颗骨珠,贯穿佩带在胸前腰间的成组的装饰品。这是至今发现随葬品中最丰富的一例。为什么这两个女孩享有如此特殊的待遇呢?既然氏族是以女性为中心,那么,一个民族内女孩的多

寡、寿夭,都直接关系着本氏族的兴旺、繁荣,姑娘的夭折,就是
本氏族最大的损失,氏族成员往往会倾尽微薄之力为他们安排
后事,举行葬礼,挑选出最精美的陶器和玩具为姑娘陪葬,使她
在另一个世界里的生活也幸福、美满,甚至将先死去的亲人的遗
骨迁入姑娘的墓穴,让他们陪伴并保护她,这一切寄托着氏族成
员的共同愿望——不要再有女孩夭折的悲剧发生,当然,对女孩
厚葬或许还有别的原因,这个女孩有一个十分特殊的身份,是氏
族的女继承人?亦或是女酋长的女儿?……

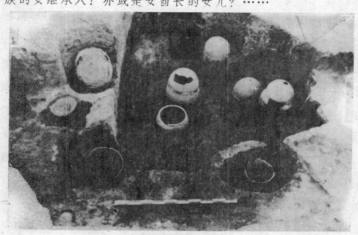

瓮棺葬群

半坡墓葬统计表

葬　　式	数　量	随葬品数量	随葬品种类
成人仰身直肢葬	153座	每座均有4件左右	陶罐、钵、尖底瓶等
成人二次葬	5座	未发现有随葬品	
成人屈肢葬	4座	1件(只有一座有随葬品)	陶　罐
成人俯身葬	15座	未发现有随葬品	
小孩瓮棺葬	78座	1件(只有一座有随葬品)	陶　罐
小孩仰身直肢葬	3座	79件(只有一座有随葬品)	陶罐、钵、尖底瓶、玉耳坠、石球、石珠

成人的葬俗

　　成人死后，一般都集中地埋在氏族的公共墓地里，在墓地中，每个家族或个人，都有他们所应占有的归宿之地；在半坡共发现成人墓葬一百七十四座，保存较好的一百一十八座，半坡的墓葬排列整齐，头部都向西或西北，安置得很有规律。那么如何解释死者的头向问题呢？在半坡时期，既没有堪舆之术，也不讲风水之俗，而是一种朴素的原始信仰支配着人们的行为，他们可能同东尼尔兰人一样，把人从生到死，看作与太阳东升西落一样，东边是新生的一边，西方是死亡的一边，人死后就随着太阳落下，所以埋葬时，背朝东，面向西，我国佤族，亦有类似的习俗，佤族认为西方就是鬼方（即鬼门的一方，太阳下落的一方），所以人死后，埋在房子附近的一边，头朝东，面向西。自然，半坡人为什么在埋葬时要将头朝西，或许与上类似，或许也有一些别的原因，例如，印度尼西亚的一些居民，埋葬死者时，将头放在西方，因为他们相信，另一鬼魂世界在西方，要通过一个洞才能进去，而这个洞要在太阳落下时，能够藉太阳的光线照亮去路，所以埋葬死者时的仪式，要在夕阳西下时举行，这样他们就相信死者便回到原来祖先所在的地方去了。

　　半坡墓葬的方式有单人独葬和多人合葬两种，单人葬，是当时流行的一种葬法，仰身直肢葬，这是当时最普遍的葬式，与近代的葬法相同，随葬品一般出在这类墓葬中，由于当时人们认为人虽然死了，但灵魂不死，在另一个世界里，会如生前一样生活，所以为死者准备了一套日常生活用品随葬，主要有吃饭的碗、汲水的瓶和壶，炊煮用的罐、盛物的盘，数量均为三——四件，值得注意的是,用工具和武器随葬的事例还不太多,可见,对当时人来说,工具、武器是十分宝贵的,人们是十分珍惜的。

墓葬中还有比较特殊的葬式:二次葬、俯身葬和屈肢葬。

二次葬是半坡氏族部落时代主要的葬俗之一。这种葬俗在原始氏族中是相当流行的,墓葬一般很规律,头向西,头骨在中间,四肢骨放置在下面或旁边,排列得都很整齐,而其葬法是人死后,先将尸体停放在一个地方,等肉体腐烂后,把骨骼收拾起来,再作第二次正式埋葬,因此,又叫"洗骨葬。"采用这种葬俗,大概是出于这种信念,即认为人的血肉是人世间的,只有等到肉体腐烂,将尸骨正式埋葬,死者才能进入鬼魂世界。据一些民族学资料来看,二次葬的仪式相当繁复,前后完成要几个月时间,今天我国台湾广东福建等地仍有此葬俗。

俯身葬,在半坡共发现七座,这种葬法,尸体作爬伏状,面向下,手臂平直放在腰的两侧,绝大多数没有随葬品。这种葬俗一直流传到殷周时代,在世界其它地区如美洲、中亚、印度及日本的北海道在古代都曾行过这种葬俗。但在各地采用这种葬俗的意义并不一致,日本北海道的虾夷人,因病死后采用俯身葬。西伯利亚的楚克契人,凡是不平常的死亡,都采用俯身葬来处理,因此在不同时代,不同地区或民族之间,各自为了特殊理由而采取同一葬法,并含有不同意义,半坡人由于什么原因采用这种葬法,难以肯定,但可以看出,它是对非正常死亡者作的特殊葬俗,在一些落后民族中,对巫师、酋长或雷电打死者,均有一定的葬法。

屈肢葬,仅见四座,一般推测其寓意为:恢复人在胎儿时的状态,因为有些部落认为"人死后埋在地腹内应当和生前在生母腹内一样躺着"。还有一种看法,可能是防止死者灵魂危害生者而加以捆绑的。

半坡的合葬墓则以两个墓为典型，一座是两个壮年男子合葬在一起，年龄约四、五十岁，身高约一米七零。另一座是四个青年女子合葬在一起，年龄约十五到二十五岁，身高一米六零左右，说到合葬墓，就使我们联想到了半坡人的婚姻情况。

人类婚姻形态的发展演进，经过了五个阶段：即杂婚、血缘婚、群婚，对偶婚及一夫一妻制。半坡正处于母系氏族公社高度发展的繁荣时期，这个时期的婚姻状况大体处于对偶婚阶段，对偶婚，是一定历史阶段的产物，它是指一对男女在或长或短的时间里比较固定的偶居，但这种偶居不是独占的同居，两性关系仍较松散，这种婚姻不稳定的根本原因在于男女双方缺乏经济上的联系，即男女双方都在各自的氏族内进行生产活动，仅保持同居关系。

半坡母系氏族公社时期，农业已有了一定程度的发展，成为社会财富来源的主要经济部门，同时，家畜饲养也作为副业应运而生，渔猎、采集虽已退居第二位，但仍是不可缺少的经济活动，当时人们在各项生产中的分工情况，大致是妇女主要从事农业生产，如播种、中耕锄草、收割、粮食加工等都由妇女承担，男子的主要工作仍是狩猎，但也开始承担例如开垦荒地，翻地松土等劳动强度较大的农活，这时男子在综合经济中的地位虽已相对提高，但仍逊于妇女，妇女仍是氏族内最有威望的首领。一个妇女在白天承担农活、家务、夜间又有许多男子来访，这对妇女来说是一个沉重负担，在这种情况下，为了适宜社会生产和婚姻生活的实际需要，在这一个时期，夜来晨去的经常变化的一男一女的走访婚，便开始向相对稳定的对偶婚转化，女娶男嫁，形成对偶家庭，共同生产，共同生活，养育子女，但经济上并不独立，依然依附于氏族或母系大家族内。

我们可以从一些民族学的资料来推测当时氏族婚姻生活的实际情景。纳西族是我国云南少数民族之一，解放前在这里，男、女社交是公开的、婚配双方，彼此称为"阿注"，"阿注"即朋友、伙伴之意。婚姻中排除母系血亲近亲的婚配，实行较严格的族外婚制。男、女白天在各自氏族中生活，与自家人一起劳动，共同生活，晚上男方就到女"阿注"那里去住宿。"阿注"之间没有共同的经济关系，在生产和生活上是分开的。这种婚姻关系很不稳定，离异是经常的，结合的时间较短，一般几个月或者一、两年。但在或长或短的时间内、男女双方都有一个固定的"阿注"，同时，还有若干个临时的"阿注"，这对双方都行之有效。而子女则跟随母亲，除在婴儿期由生母在正房哺乳外，平时跟祖母生活在一起，住在公共居住的大房屋内，由于子女不跟父亲生活在一起，所以，只知其母，不知其父，在亲属称谓中，也没有专用的父称。客房是供女子在夜间接待男子用的，客房的数目和家庭已婚女子的数目相吻合，白天已婚女子除了从事生产活动外，一般都在正房内活动，晚饭后才回到自己的客房，等候男"阿注"的到来。男女双方合则留，不合则去，也可能几个男子同时爱上一个女子，但决不会因此打架生事。妇女在家庭中支配一切，一个男子，无论在一个家庭中拥有多少子女或占有多少财产，都要随时听候命令，准备离开这个家庭。纳西族的这种婚姻关系给了我们类比地理解远古时代母系氏族社会的一把钥匙。

半坡的葬俗中除发现以上提到的两座女性四人合葬和男性二人合葬外，其余都是单人葬，单人葬和同性合葬的葬俗都是母系氏族实行族外婚的反映：由于本氏族内兄弟姊妹不通婚，兄弟必须出嫁，在别的氏族中寻找妻子，出嫁的男子死后，又都分别归葬于各自的出生氏族,而按照氏族内不许通婚的制度,他们也不能同本氏族的姊妹同墓合葬。同时,由于姊妹只能从外民族娶夫进来,他们死后同样不能同本氏族的兄弟合葬,但同性合葬、男女分别埋葬,则是许可的,因此,也就不难理解为什么在半坡只有成年同性合葬而未见成年异性合葬了。半坡墓地中的两个男性合葬墓和四个女性合葬墓中的死者,由于他们各自的年龄都较相近,因此,他们的关系应属于同一辈份的兄弟或姐妹,而且,合葬墓中的死者都为一次葬,即他们大致是在同时或相距不久的时间内死去的,这难道是巧合吗?过去在侗族有这种情况,即成人死后不立即埋葬,而是将死者装入棺材,停放于村寨附近的一个地方待本寨中与死者同一年出生或同一辈份的人死光之后再择定吉日一同埋葬,这使我们理解半坡合葬墓得到启发,半坡同性合葬中的死者不仅辈份相同,而且,很可能还是同一年出生的同龄者,这是因为在古代一些氏族部落中,人们出于一种原始宗教意识的考虑,以为同一氏族或家族中同年出生的兄弟或姊妹,他们既然是在同一年中由阴世投身到阳世中来,那么他们也应当在同一年中再结伴一同返回到阴界中去,一旦他们当中有人死去,其他的同龄伙伴便情愿殉死,借以达到同归的目的。看来,半坡墓地这种合葬习俗的含义可能正是如此。

在半坡墓葬中还有一个十分普遍的现象,就是随葬品中一部分陶器口部是被有意打破的,其用意何在呢?原来,在他们看来,阴界同阳界正好相反,只有将食具摔碎后随葬,死者在阴界才能得到完整的用品,可见半坡人不仅灵魂观念相当复杂,而且阴阳两界观念也是相当复杂的。半坡的葬俗可能还有更为深刻的含义,这些都等待着有心者的耕耘。

从半坡先民原始母系氏族社会的遗址中,我们仿佛看到了中华民族的祖先在六、七千年前在这里辛勤劳作,繁衍生息的情景,那盆盆罐罐、断壁残垣莫不凝结着先民对美好生活的憧憬、向往,当看到半坡人创造的灿烂的古代文化时,每一个黄皮肤的中国人怎能不深感骄傲,又怎能不为祖先的奋斗精神所打动呢?正是从这里升起了中华民族文明的第一道曙光,也从这里,我们看到了明天——中国的明天——一个大有希望的明天。

单人葬

BANPO
MATRIARCHAL SOCIETY

英文翻译　李长平　曹学品

审　　定　朱景琪　赵　起

BANPO MATRIARCHAL SOCIETY

CATALOGUE

Preface

The Banpo site is located on the second terrace on the east bank of Chan River, eastern suburb of Xi'an. It preserves a complete and typical sample of Matriarchal clan society which existed in Yellow River 6,700 years ago. The site was discovered in 1953. With the five excavations from 1954 to 1957, nearly 10,000 relics were unearthed. The site covers an area of more than 10,000 square metres which is one fifth of the total square. In 1958, the first museum of Neolithic site were founded in China. It is well known as the Museum of Bampo Site. In order to popularize the knowledge of clan society,《Banpo Matriarchal Clan Society》analyzes the production, consciousness, life style, as well society system of the Banpo people in a easy way, The sources of its materials are based on ruins and relics from the site and the result of National Study.

I . The Surroundings of the Banpo People

If human beings want to survive, they need, first of all ,a suitable environment, The reason why the Banpo people could settle down and live on is due to the fact that they profited, to a great extent, from the fine natural environment along the Yellow River.

Shaanxi is situated in the middle and the lower reaches of the Yellow River, the Wei River flowing across with tributaries densely covered on both sides, the land being fertile, and called 800 Li Qin Plain in its history, a good place ever since the ancient time where human beings multiplied as well as a place which was the birthplace of the famous Yangshao Culture,

To the west side of the Banpo site, flows the Chan River, one of the renowned eight rivers around the ancient capital Chang'an and an affluent of the Wei River, 6000 years ago, the Chan River did not rise or fall suddenly and violently as it does today with its plentiful water overflowing now and then, thus leaving many lakes and marshes on its banks as a result, the Banpo people were never worried about the supply of water.

Next to the east side of the Banpo site, lies the White Deer Plain, and to the south lies the Zhongnan Mountains. 6000 years ago, primeval forests grew densely, where all sorts of birds and beasts appeared and disappeared. It turned out that through the studies of the sporepollenin of the soil of the Banpo site, such a conclusion can be drawn: the climate at the time when the Banpo people were living there was warmer and more humid than it is today, similar to that at today's Hanzhong of southern Shaanxi, its annual average temperature was 4 degrees centigrade higher than it is today, The thick forests and the beasts haunting them provided the Banpo people with an excellent place for gathering and hunting. To the northern side of the Banpo site, lies the Wei River Plain, an ideal place for human beings to be engaged in the primitive agriculture.

II. Figures and Facial Features of the Banpo People

According to the studies conducted by scholars, the Banpo people belonged to the southern Mongolian race, with similar characteristics in physique as the southern Chinse, having developed by dirctly inheriting the blood relationship of the Upper Cave Man, thus being the lineal ancestors of the Chinese nation, with their skin as the representative of the ancestors of the yellow race. Their prominent and protruding cheekbones, their spade — shaped incisors which were recessed from the inside, displayed the typical features of the yellow race. The Banpo people also had high foreheads, flat and straight noses, as well as lips with moderate thickness. In a word, they had both the characteristics of northerners and some features of southerners.

Then what about their height? According to the Chinese popular legend, the ancient people enjoyed extradinary height, for example, they stood eight feet high , or they topped ten feet, etc. However, this does not tally with facts. Considering the changes in relation to the historical physique of human beings in the past 2,000,000 years, the human height has not changed from tall to short, but from short to tall gradually. From the analysis of a large number of human skeletons discovered at the Banpo site, the Banpo man was about 170 cm in statue, equaling the average height of modern people. At the same time, the cerebral cubic measure of the Banpo people was 1376 ml, approximating 1400 ml of the modern people. The Banpo people possessed equally developed intelligence as the modern people. Therefore, anthropololgists have pointed out that the Banpo people and the modern people belong to the same race of homo sapiens.

III. The Agricultural Production and the Raising of Domestic Animals of the Banpo Clan

The Banpo people were richly endowed by nature in their

natural environment and geographical conditions for their engagement in the agricultural production . The Banpo area was warmer and more moist 6,000 years ago than it is today, with forests, plains, marshes and rivers. Fishes were produced in the water areas. In such surroundings, there existed the convenience of collection and fishing with the advantage of farming. Of course, people depended on Heaven for food, going in for dry farming, since there were no man — made irrigation faciltites yet.

The main crop unearthed from the Banpo site was millet. Millet seeds were discovered in a stean. Such a crop had its advantages: drought tolerance, thus suitable for growing in the loess areas of northern China; simple techniques were required in its production; a bigger harvest yield; a shorter mature period; long period of storage without getting rotten. Hence the main crop of the north at that time.

Then, what about the source of the millet? It turned out that at the early stage of human beings, common labour and life united them. Determined by the natural division of labour, men were engaged in hunting, fishing and other heavy physical labour, whereas women were involved in collections, in the long course of which women gradually mastered the laws of the growing of plants, thus acclimatizing green bristlegrass which became a crop domesticated by people.

The coming into being of millets made it possible for human beings to settle down. The Banpo people used the slash and burn farming method, cutting down trees and weeds with stone axes, burning them with fire, thus turning plant ashes into fertilizer and opening up wild land into cultivated fields. The stone axes they used underwent a process of development. No holes were drilled in the earlier stone axes. They were fixed between the two pieces which were cut at the end of the handle and bound with ropes. However, this could not make the stone axes steady. Later, stone axes with drilled holes were invented thus overcoming this disadvantage. As a result, the efficiency of production was promote, and the stone axes were themselves very fine handicraft articles. Though stone axes with drilled holes had been invented, it might be imagined that the efficiency in cutting down trees with stone axes was still very low. Nevertheless, before the metal tools came out, stone implements were the main implements in production, indispensable in felling trees, opening up cultivated fields, of building houses and other aspects. They accompanied human beings for over a mxillion years, going through the Stone Age in archaeology. Of course, the Banpo clan might have adopted other methods, such as the method used by a northern American clan with the men taking barks off huge trees in the first year, so that the trees would wither, and burning the trees in the following year.

After the crop had grown in the previous year on the soil, it had to be turned up so as to make up for soil fertility so that the crop could grow in the following year. The main tool in turning up the soil was stonespade, which was similar to the modern iron spade. Besides , there were bone spades made of shoulder blades of animals. The sowig was broadcast. A fter sowing, the Banpo people used stone hoes to cover the soil. The stone hoes are similar to the modern picks. They were made by knocking with the heads a bit sharper or thin and round, the body longer and fixed at the wooden handles. They might also be used for weeding.

When autumn came, people used stone knives or pottery knives for harvests. At both sides of the stone knives, there were notches, between which ropes might be tied, so that people could insert their thumbs to hold while using them. In the later period, stone knives with handles fixed to them were invented.

The method of grain processing used by the Banpo people had reached a certain level. At the site stone grinders and stone grinding clubs were discovered. When they used them, millets were put on the grinding stone, and then the millets were ground with stone clubs by hands, for peeling the millets or grinding them into flour. Tools for processing were very primitive. However, in the Feiligang Culture, which was one or two thousand years earlier than the Banpo clan, big and refined stone grinder had been used with four feet underneath. Why was it so? As a matter of fact, viewing from the data of ethnoiogy, the most primitive instrument of processing was the stone grinder. Later stone pestles and wooden mortars came into existence. Since the Banpo people had used mortars and pestles which were comparatively more advanced, stone grinderes became secondary.

All this shows that the Banpo people had reaped a whole set of experience in agricultural production from reclaiming the fields, to loosening the soil for sowing, to harvests when the crops were ripe, as well as to grain processing.

During the period of the Banpo clan, people also began growing vegetables. Seeds of vegetables were discovered in a pottery jar for storage, seeds which had carbonized. Scientific appraisal has proved that they are the seeds of Chinese cabbages or leaf mustards. Vegetables were a kind of non — staple foodstuffs. Undoubtedly, their growing enriched the material life of the Banpo people.

In the course of excavation, archaeologists have also discovered two sites of sheep pens and pigsties, and the bones of six animals of pigs, dogs, oxen, sheep, horses and chickens. According to the studies of the experts on the history of the raising of animals, the only domestic animals which could be determined were pigs and dogs. It is estimated that oxen, sheep, horses and chickens were being tamed.

The raising of domestic animals developed along with the long — settled life. It may be understood that with the emergence of a settled life, the sources of people's food became steady gradually. They got extra animals for their food, and so they managed to raise them for future food. Therefore a new branch of economy came into being — the raising of domestic animals.

IV. Hunting, Fishing and Collection

Hunting

Hunting economy played a rather important role in the life of the Banpo people. It not only provided people with meat, but also supplied them with other daily necessitise such as fur, bones, horns, and oil, Around the living quarters were meadows and marshes as well as dense jungles. There were a large number of wild animals. It may be judged from the bones of animals discovered at the site that they were barred deer, red deer, bamboo rats, racoon dogs, badgers, foxes, rabbits, rocs and so on , most of which were the bones of barred deer. Hunting activities were conducted collectively. The tools for hunting were arrows, stone balls, stone spears etc.

Arrows were the major implenments of hunting.

Fishing

Fishing was also an important occupation in the economic sectors of the Banpo inhabitants. The barbed fish — hooks and barbed harpoons invented by them were exquisitely made and Looked as beautiful as the present — day metal ones. The way they fished was similar to that of ours today. It is estimated that harpooning was more popular than fishing in those days.

Although no trace of the fishing — nets has been found, the cord and fish patterns on the unearthed painted pottery utensils still demonstrate the inhabitants' use of fishing — nets. They presumably made fishingnets with hemp ropes. Of course they might fish by drying a certain fishing ground.

In the course of fishing, one person's strength was too weak, the inhabitants had to work in close coordination, and therefore group action became dominant. In fishing season, the inhabitants of the whole village would go out, working together and sharing the bitter and sweets of working.

Collection

Primitive agriculture could not guarantee sufficient daily necessities. The inhabitants would get food from nature——"the natural storehouse,"They gathered pine nuts, chestnuts, hazel nuts and so on. The shells and spiral shells discovered at the site have proved that. At that time, women were usually responsible for gathering food. Veteran women would go out with children to gather food in slack season.

As you know, in order to get the necessities for survival, the inhabitants had to engage in various forms of production. Otherwise they could not survive.

V. The style of eating together

How did the inhabitants distribute the food once they got

it? In the time of Banpo Clan Community, both land and produce belonged to all the members of the community. What they got through hard working was the common wealth of the community—— that is everyone could get a share of it.

Some of the data on ethnology shows that the most strict communist food distribution was prevailing at the time of Banpo. Everyone should comply with the rules

For instance, in some Indian tribes, all the fish were put together for keeping in store. Every evening each woman could get the same amount as the others could get, for the distribution was carrried out according to the total number of women in the tribe. In the native tribes in Central America, food—— the most important thing among their property was by no means controled by anyone or any clan. The meat of the animals they hunted was evenly distributed according to the different rules in different tribes.

Take the aboriginals on Island for example, once in year of famine, they would go to the sea to look for food. If someone happened to find a run—aground whale, which was his favorite food, he would, first of all, tell all the members in his tribe about what he had found, instead of eating it himself, although he himself was starving. The whale would be distributed equitably among the members by the aged. As for the Eskimos, when they carried out the distribution, everyone would be on the list, especially the sick and widows without children, even if they had only one piece of meat. From above facts we may certainly infer that the Banpo inhabitants also adopted the way of distribution that was same to that of the aboriginals in America, because all the inhabitants were equally treated also.

As a result of low productivity and lack of produce at the time, food — sharing became very prevalant. In those days, apart from facing sheer poverty the inhabitants, from time to time, would go suffer from ailments and even be killed in some unexpected disasters.

Scientific analysis of the remains of 150 adults discovered at the site shows that their average age was only 30 years. One third of those burried in the cemetery were children. Many of them died very young. Some even died as soon as they were born. From this we can see that the conditions of life were extremely poor. Therefore, only when the rigid equitable distribution was carried out, could they get a share of the fruits of their labour, maintain their poor living standard, and get involved in production in high spirits. Otherwise, some of them would die of hunger, and group strength would be weakened.

VI. Clothing Style of the Banpo Inhabitants

The Banpo inhabitants had already developed their own clothing style with the sense of primitive esthetic judgement.

The inventions of bone shuttles and stone spinning wheels convinced us that the clever Banpo inhabitants had a good grasp of weaving skills. They would spin the fibers of some wild plants such as hemp and kudzu vine into thread and then make cloth with the thread. The primitive loom was flat. Before weaving, the weaver would fix one end of the warp to the machine firmly, and the other end to the waist and then throw the shuttle from rignt to left repeatedly to make cloth. The visible impression left at the bottom of some pottery utensils show that cloth woven by the Banpo inhabitants look very much like gunnysack, almost as fine as the present — day canvas. The 281 bone needles of delicate workmanship discovered at the site with eyes at their ends which made it possible to pass thread through them. This shows that Banpo inhabitants had already gotten the hang of sewing.

According to archeological and ethnological data, we infer that the stylizde clothes did not come into being at the time of Banpo. The coats and pants was not evidently divided Their clothes had neither collars nor sleaves. The way they dressed themselves was to put some pieces of flax cloth on and fasten it at the waists. The appearance of cloth was not only for preventing cold, but also for beautifying themselves as well.

Banpo women, 6,000 to 7,000 years ago, were very good at making themselves look prettier. Different sorts of ornamental objects and clothes have been unearthed at the site. They fall roughly into two groups according to their shapes and functions. Some of them are rings, beads, pendants, and some of them are ornamental pieces for the neck, head, waist, the decorative pieces set in their clothes. There ornamental objects relevent to different parts of their bodies. The materials for making the objects cover a wide range, including pottery, jade, stone ,bone, animal horns and shells etc. The found remains at the cemetery shows that women mostly wore the ornamental pieces which were always suitable for such occasions as weaving,pottery — making and farming. The sight of them would please the eye,and take their mind off their work.

VII. Daily Utensils

Banpo people left us a large number of differently shaped pottery wares which they used in their daily life.

Talking about pottery wares, it is necessary to mention the invention of it. At the very beginning, to make the containers fireproof the people applied damp clay to the outer surface of the woven weed or wooden containers, then put them on fire to cook food. As a result, the woven weed or wooden container were burned. What remained became well— shaped containers. That's the story about the the people's accidental invention of pottery wares.

Banpo people's skills in pottery making gradually improved. The utensils they produced look exquistely beautiful. However, the low productivity kept their skill in manual stage. Two main methods were used in the pottery making:

1)shaping by hand 2) shaping by colling the damp clay. The first way they did it was to make the damp rope of clay into the wanted shape by coiling it.

The finished products would be small with thinner walls. The second way they did it was to place the damp clay pieces one ring upon another or to pile them up piece by piece.

A lot of additional work was reqired to made the half — finished vessels look prettier. Take the big urn for example, additional damp caly pieces would be added somewhere to its middle parts which were protruding not only for decoration but also for strengtening the wall of the vessel and for the practical usage as well. The potter had already taken that ino consideration, before he started making it.

At last, the finished clay vessels would be sent to kilns for firing. The pottery making area is located at the eastern part of Banpo village where six intact kilns have been discovered. We infer from their size that the kilns then were not big. One could only a couple of unbaked caly vessels, or two or three dozens of smaller ones, or one or two big ones.

Banpo kilns are the oldest ones in China. They are divided into two kinds, interms of their structures. One is the horizontal kiln and the other is the vertical kiln. Each of the kilns consists of a fire chamber, a fire passage, a fire grate and kiln chamber. The horizontal kilns were the earliest ones used by the Banpo people. Each was built with a fire chamber shaped like a big tilted tube about 200 meters long with the kiln chamber resting on the top part. Right behind the tilted fire chamber, was the kiln chamber shaped like a sky line with a diameter of one meter. The place between the fire chamber and the kiln chamber was the fire grate where the unbaked pottery vessels were placed. There were three passages inside the kiln. One was in the center, the other two, one on each side. There were some square or round holes arrangeed in a circle which shared the equidistance between them. The holes in the grate closer to the fire chamber were small and those farther from it were bigger, so that the kiln temperature could be regulated and the claywares could be evenly baked.

The vertical kilns which began to appear in the later period of Banpo were more advanced in structure than their precursers. A marked characteristic of the vertical kiln was that the fire passage was much closer to the kiln chamber shaped like a big bag with the fire chamber just below it. There were two big holes under the grate which served as the fire channels. Generally speaking, the kiln was larger in size than any of its forerunners.

Fire wood was the major fuel for baking the pottery. Scientific appraisal have proved that the temperature could reach 800 c — —1,000 C. Most of the baked pottery wares looked beautiful in color.

Banpo people made different varieties of pottery untensils covering most of the present — day selections of pottery. In terms of usage, they were divided into several kinds, including food and water containers and containers for storing things. The main kitchen utensils included bowls, basins, etc. There were some containers looking like the present — day goblest. Different vessels served different purposes in daily life. They present us with the diversified ways of life of the ancient people.

One of the most important pieces of the kitchen utensils was the pottery steamer looking like a basin or a bowl bearing some square or round holes in its bottom. It was used with a pot and a cover as a whole set. When cooking, the steamer was first placed inside the pot with water in it and then heated. After the water boiled for a specific period of time, the food would be well done. That very thing was the precurser of the present day steamer. As early as 6,000 to 7,000 years ago, the Banpo people began to take advantage of steam.

The water containers mainly included bottles with pointed bases, gourd — shaped vases, flasks and pot with a spout like opening on its rim.

The bottle with pointed base was used for getting water. It has a short neck, a big belly and a plinted base with two ears on both sides, theory looking involved like an olive at first sight. Some scientific theory was involed in making the bottle. The stream line on the surface of the bottle is clear. It never leaks, once filled with water no matter how violently it is shaken, because the rim was narrow enough to keep the water inside it. With a big belly it contains more water. The pointed base can decentralize the water pressure on the base. You can tie a rope to the two side ears. People can either carry it on the shoulder or on the back. It makes it easier for the old and young to carry water.

The way it works is interesting. When fetching , you put the bottle in water, it will take a horizontal position on the surface, the water goes into it naturally as it filled with water, it goes back to vertical position scientific appraisle has proved that the way by which the bottle was filled up with water was closely associated with the principle of the center gravity.

By imitating the shape of the natural gourd, the Banpo people made pretty gourd — shaped bottles which were very convenient for the hunters to carry when going hunting. It was as good as the present day military portable water bottles. The earliest gourd — shaped bottle was the very copy of the natural gourd. Later, the people gradually got rid of copying gourd, and made another kind of water container—the flask by changing shape of the gourd. Its rim was wider than its neck with the upper part of the belly jutting out a little bit and with the lower part sunken a bit. Its perfect symmetry is harmonized by its arc — shaped design. Its curved lines add to the glamor of it.

The sight of the pottery container with a spout on its rim reminds us of the present — day tea pot. The protruding part on the rim, which is called"Liu" in Chinese (meaning a thing from which liquids pours), is equivalant to today's spout of teapot. It makes the liquids pour easier. The big pottery jars vats were used as food and water containers. The walls of the vessels were even a solid, showing the high skills of the professional potters in pottery manufacturing.

In the course of manufacturing the pottery, the potters accumulated a great deal of experience. As a result, a solid foundation was laid for the development of the handicraft industry, which later gradually became independent from agriculture. As you know, in addition to Banpo, nine out of all the archeological sites of Yangshao Culture were discovered in Guanzhong area where the earliest Chinese people lived and worked.

VIII. Sculpted and Painted Signs

During the course of excavation, some 113 in 22 forms of simple signs were discovered, which were sculpted or painted below the rims of some pottery basins. To be exact, the signs were sculpted or painted in side the belt—shaped patterns and upsidedown triangles. The strokes of all the signs look graceful and regular, in terms of their type. They look very much like the earlier script carved on bones or tortoise shells of the Shang Dynasty. Moreover, in addition to Banpo, nine other sites of Yangshao Culture were also discovered in Guangzhong area. That is to say all the sculpted and painted signs originat-

ing in Yangshao Culture are most probably the precurser of
the sculpted carved on bones or tortoise shells.

IX . Painted Pottery Wares of Banpo

The Banpo people made a large number of painted pottery
vessels with beautiful, colorful patterns and graceful strokes.
The simple artist designs with profound meaning reflect the
rich spiritual life of the people of Banpo Clan Community.

The painted pottery wares of Banpo are of fine quality and
have smooth surfaces. A part from the red and white colors, a
lot of black color was used, which, with the manganese diox-
ided as coloring agent, could offer a sharp contrast. Dark colors painted on the smooth surface of the fine clay vessels look
more on the smooth surface of the fine clay vessels look more
on the smooth surface of the fine clay vessels look more attractive. To achieve artistic harmony, the Banpo people knew
what kind of paintings they should paint on the vessels by
looking at their shapes. On the inner walls or on the protruding parts of the vessels which people often set their eyes on are
mostly painted human face, fish, deer, impression of fishing
nets and so on. The upper parts of the vessels are dotted with
geometric patterns arranged in four units in a circle. Smaller
painted pottery vessels like the narrow — necked flasks were
perfectly designed. From a higher or a lower position in which

you put them you get a different visual impression. When designing them, the potter took the artistic and visual efects into consideration. When you look directly at the upper part of a pottery tea pot, you'll find it looks something like a when you over look at it, you'll feel it looks like a blooming flower, the rim of which looks like a stamen. Some of the combinations of the decorative patterns on the pottery wares are dark and some are bright, some are big and some are small, some are black and some are white, some are simple and some are complicated. However, thery are all in aesthetie harmony. The harmonious sense of the patterns and designs always refresh yourself as soon as you see them. The practicality of them can not be separated from harmony which reflects the improved aesthetie standard of the people.

The paintd pottery wares themselves have regular shapes and a compact texture, but the geometric designs, ornamental patterns, on them have a very strong sense of decoration. The earliest geometric patterns and designs on the painted pottery wares came from those of the woven articles. In the course of a long period of development, in terms of designing, they gradually got away from the primitive way of copying the images of objects. Later, more new patterns and designs involved from the former ones, which gave you only the abstract impressions of real objects.

The imitative patterns of animals and plants are specially done with profound symbolic and mysterious meanings, including fish patterns, deer patterns and human face patterns etc. of which the fish patterns come first in number. The fish patterns went through all the ages of the Yangshao Culture and were representative designs of the painted pottery utensils.

With a simple artistic style most of the fish designs are realistic and single ones. The head of the fish. including the gills, the fins, tail and the body was done in detail (its teeth are noticable). The simple design gives you the sense of how simple, how naive it is.

In the later period of Banpo some artistic exageration was used when doing a fish. In stead of painting a fish in detail on a vessel, they would paint only part of a fish to show it was fish. Hence the triangle served as the fish head and the dot in the middle of it served as the eye. It shows the evolution of the artistic style of Banpo people—from true-to-life to abstract from realistic to freehand.

Only a few of the unearthed pottery utensils bear deer designs. In a basin four small deer were found on the inner wall, standing there looking alert, getting ready to avoid catastrophe, as if the enemy were approaching. The images of deer were done in detail, vivid to life, with the style of traditional Chinese paintings.

The painted pottery basin with mermaid design

The design is a combination of a human head and a fish body. The round head with an *ornamental piece* on it, has long crescent brows, closed eyes looking like short segments of a line, a nose looking like an upside down "J", a big mouth indicated by a triangle and ears represented by two small fish. The human face and the fish body were joined together with perfect artistic exageration.

Origionally, the mermaid pattern didn't exist in the world. Later it came into being. What on earth did this strange thing represent? It is estimated that Banpo people believed that the ansesters their clan originated from were fish, they were fond of fish and then fish became the totem of their clan. One ancient Chinese myth tells the story about how a fish transformed itself into a human being.

In the childhood of human being people could not give the correct explaination to their own. Some of things that nature could offer people were as rainstorm with thunders and lightings, inundation and earthquake. They did frighten people. People at that time could not understand them. So they turned to what they thought the protective objects of spiritual aspirations such as mountain, water, plants ans so on. Therefore, in the course of the clanss' development, they would take fierce animals and other animals with special functions as their protective gods. A clan would take a particular plant or animal as the image of their ancestor and then they worship it. Hence the worship of totem.

At the time of Banpo, the clan communities were very prosporous. And under that social system the worship of totem became very popular.

The motifs of fish, deer in the pottery vessels of Banpo are probably associated with totems. It would be reasonable to think that the Banpo clan's totem was symbolized by the mermaid motif.

Up to this day, some minority people still worship animals. For example, the people of the Bai Nationality took fish and conches as their burial objects. Undoutedly, this practice was derived from the worship of animals. Fish tail — shaped scarves have been always fashionable among the women of the Bai nationality. The scarves were also derived from the ritual activities of worshiping fish.

In remote ancient times, clans were named after creatures and other living things. For instance, there were You Shi, Shennong Shi, Shenlong Shi, Xiong Shi and so on which had relations with animals and plants. The people of the Han nationality took Ma (horse) Niu (cattle), Li(plum), Mei(intersweet), Lin (woods),etc. as their family names respectively. Those are the origin of totems. The people of the Gaoshan nationality in Taiwan take snake and pottery vessels as their totems . The people of the Yao and the She nationalities take dog as their totems, all of which resulted in animal worship.

In a word, the Banpo people probably believed hat their ancestors were fish or humanized creaturesas with the fish bodies and human faces.

X. The simple-naive-ancient -looking Pottery Figures and Their Charm

The simple—ancient looking figurines made by the Banpo were beautifully modeled . They are usually praised as the treasures of the primitive arts.

Most of figurines were shaped according to the images of the most familiar domestie animals they raised in those days. The figurines of birds and animals of Banpo served mainly as the knobs of the lids of the pottery containers. The bird's outline is distinct. It's head and neck suggest that it looks like a pigeon. In a standing position, the animal has a head of a beast and tail of a bird. It would be very interesting, if you get a closer look a it, because its face bears the resemblance to both a dog and a goat. Modeled out of clay by hand, the human head is slightly flat with a square face, a big nose, a pair of big ears, and two deeply sunken eyes which are extra pieces of clay added to the face when soft. There are two holes. one in each of the ears. It was used as a decorative piece or a child's toy. Being closely associated with the ancient people, the human head reflected the ability and knowledge in artistic expression of the Banpo people.

The other two attractive articles of Banpo are the clay whistles known as "magic flutes". They were the earlist melodious holed wind instrument. Each of the two was meticulously modeled, on which more than two notes could be played. The scale, tone and timbre sound very much like the music in Qin Opera (the local opera of Shaanxi Province). It is believed that the whistles are the testimony of the Qin music. (Shaanxi is called Qin for short). More than 6,000 to 7,000 years ago, the whistles might be used to give signals to each other.

XI. The Layout of Banpo Village and the Structure of the Houses

Banpo is one of the largest village of Yanshao Culture. It covers an area of 50,000 square meters, comprising three parts: the habitation area; the pottery manufacturing center and the cemetery. The size of the habitation area is 30,000 square meters. One fifth of the whole village (an area of 10,000 square meters) has been excavated, with a surrounding moat about 5 meters deep and 6 meters wide. The cemetery is located north of the moat. To the east of the moat is the pottery manufacturing center. The distribution of the habitation area, the potttery manufacturing center and the cemetery reflects Banpo people's ideas of planning. After systmatic excavation in the habitation area, the items discovered include the remains of 46 houses, over 200 storage pits, two pens for domestic animals, 73 children's burial jars, and more than 10,000 pieces of production tools etc. Excavations on the site suggest that the village was planned in good order.

A 160 sq. m. large house was found in the center of the village with smaller houses built around it. The doors of the smaller houses were open toward the largest one in the center, making up a cohesive layout. The importance of the large house can find its expression at its own location.

According to the ethnolgical data, we infer that the large house was reserved for the children and the aged and also for religous and ritual activities. When a man came of age, the ceremony marking his reaching adulthood was also held there. After that he would move out from the large house to his spouse's house in another clan. Hence the large house was the cradle of the clan members, so to speak. At the same time, it also served as the meetingroom where the people had discussions, distributed products among themselves and elected the chief of their clan or tribe.

The circular layout of the habitation area was based on the principle of cohesion. At that time, all the clan members were united by lineage. Everyone's life depended on the clan.

The average size of the small houses is about 20 squqre meters. In terms of the shape, the houses unearthed on the site may be divided into two groups: round ones and square ones. As far as the structure is concerned, they may be divided into two types: semi— underground houses and the ones on the ground. Each house has a fireplace in its center for cooking, heating and aluminating purposes. Between the entrance and firepit there is a square threshold to stop rain. In side the house, the walls and the floor were make of mud mixed with straw and smoothed when soft. All the houses shared equidistance and were regularly arrayed.

The square houses were mostly semi — underground. They way it was built was that the builders would dig up a square pit the inside of which would serve as walls. And then they put up a roof over it and moved in. You may wonder why the people built their houses that way? This is because people just moved to the plain front caves and they didn't know how to make walls when they built houses. But, it would be much easier for them to dig up a pit and to let the inside of the pit serve as walls of the house. It was damp and dark inside the house, for it was deep in the ground.

In the later period of Banpo, there was usually a sleeping platform on the left hand side in a square house which covered half of it. The other half was used for keeping food and utensils. Apparently, by the later period of Banpo all the things inside the houses had already been reasonably arranged.

Square houses built up above the ground were rare. But there was a very typical one which was thought to be the most advanced type by the Banpo standard, because the ways it was built were more complicated architecturally. All the 20 wooden columns propping the house were placed in three rows having four in each, buried half a meter deep in the ground and all architecturally arranged. After the pillars were buried, the rafters would be placed to form the tow — sloped roofs. Whth erect walls and slant roofs, the house set a good example for furture arthitectures. The traditional Chinese architectural style was derived from that type of house.

One kind of the round houses was put up with wooden framework. Another kind of the round houses was semi — underground. The former looked like a Mongolian yurt, the latter looked like a cone with its top cut offf. That kind of houses were put up with big coloums, thick rafters and lots of mud. In traditional Chinese architecture, the front part of a house usually serves as the sittingroom and the rear part serves as the bedrooms.

The thresholds in the earlier houses at Banpo were built only to prevent rain and the huts over the dwelling pits were used to avoid rainstorm or snowstorm. And the entrance and the hut was the precurser of the sittingroom. Further inside the house two dark rooms were divided by the partition wall. From the structure of those earlier houses, later the traditional architects developed the traditional style of Chinese architecture.

If you look at the house from left to right, you'll find that the partition divides the house into two parts — the front and the rear, hence "the front sittingroom and the rear bedroom style". The construction of the ancient palaces also followed the same exmple of Banpo — — the front part served as the meeting room and the rear part served as the bedrooms reserve for the emperors and their consorts.

XII. Burial custom and its thought, belief, marriage feature, ideology.

The funeral custom prevailed among the Banpo people reflected their spiritual life. They were all pious religious believers, so to say. They not only conducted ritual and other religious activities concerning agriculture, but also worship in a faithful fashion the totem— the symbol of their clan. There were also many rigid rules and complicated ways to bury the dead. The intact skeletons unearthed at the site and variation in the ways that they were buried was really unique.

A. The Children's Burial Custom

When the adult died, they were usually buried in the cemetery of their clan. However the dead children were buried in a very special way. A child who died young was usually put in a pottery jar and then buried somewhere near the house. Some were put in big jars covered with pottery basins. For the teenagers, their remians would be put in big jars covered the same ones of the same size. The children and the adults were never buried together in those days. The same cases have been found in some archeological and ethnological data. The aobigionals on the Adman Island would bury the dead adult outside their village. But the dead children would be buried beneath their houses. A dead adult of the Wa people in China would be buried in a certain place in the cemetery according to his or her family name. But a dead child would be rolled up in a bamboo mat without any burial objects and buried somewhere near the house. The Yao people in Lian Nan autonomous county in Guangdong Province would bury the dead of the same clan in tomb shaped tombs to show their flesh — and — blood ties with the dead. However, the dead children were not allowed to be buried in the cemetery. According to their usual pratice, when an infant less than a month old died, it would be buried in the ground somewhere under the mother's bed. This is because they believe that the infant died so young that they still needed to be taken care of by its parents. It would be a great worry to bury it outside.

In Yaoshan Town of Libo County in Guizhou Province, there's another group of Yao people whose ancestors prefered burying the dead in caves. Before 1949, they already switch to burying the dead in tombs. According to their usual practice. however, the dhildren under ten years of age would be buried somewhere in the lowest place around the village than being placed in coffins and buried in the cemetery.

The difference in the ways the adult and the children were buried depended mostly on their own age. In another word, the people's ages were closely associated with the ways they were buried. Take the Xina people in Yunnan Province for example, before liberation, when a boy or a girl was 13 years old, a kind of ceremony known as "putting a pair of pants on him or putting a skirt on her" would be held to mark their into the adulthood.

In the past, the practice of the Bulang people of Yunnan province was that a special ceremony was held in which the boys and girls who came of age would dye each other's teeth black with the ashes remained from a kind of burned tree. Actually it was the ceremony which marked the beginning of their adulthood. That is to say they began to turn a new page in their life one after another. To be exact they were allowed to date.

From the above facts we learned that the mother's tender love and great concern for her child can find its best expression in the dhildren's burial jars at Banpo. If a child died young, then its mother would bury it beside the houes, for she hated to see her child being hurt by the wild beasts. The children for whom the adulthood ceremony were not held were not regarded to be as members of the clan. That's why the Banpo adults buried their chilren in somewhere else rather than in the cemetery.[1]

It is noticable that most of the pottery bowls or basins that served as the covers of burial jars had holes right in the middle of the bottoms. Why the Banpo people drilled those holes? As a matter of fact, drilling small holes purposely on pottery burial jars was not the only custom at Banpo. It had been popular among some ethnic groups in China by the days of liberation. For example, cremation was among some Tibeten people who lived in Heyuan town, Mianning county, Sichuan Province. After the dead were cremated, their ashes would be put into burial jars with small holes in their covers. They meant to let the souls of the dead go out to the other world. Although some other ethnic people didn't drill holes in their coffins, they still drilled holes in their tombs or placed a door inside it. Some people drilled a hole in the upper left — hand part of the tomb to make it available to worship the dead. After they finished the worshiping, the sacrificial offerings would be put into the hole for the dead to eat. The holes in the burial jars at Banpo also served as passages for the souls of the dead.

B. The Adults Funeral

At the time of Banpo, the dead adults would be collectively buried in the cemetery of their clan. The excavated 170 tombs at Banpo reveal that the remians of the dead were all arranged in good order. they were placed inside their tombs with their head facing the west. Motivated by the simple premitive religions ideas, they believed that a person's life span was equivalent to the rise and set of the sun. That's why the Banpo people buried the dead with their faces to the west and their backs to the east.

There were two main ways to buried the dead at Banpo. One was burying the remains of a single person in the cemetery; another was burying the remains of a couple of persons together. The former way was more preferable at Banpo, which was smimilar to the way that is prevailing today.

The remains of the dead were found to be with various postures. Some were buried with their faces up and arms and legs straight and some were buried with their faces down and some were buried sideway.

Most of the burial objects were unearthed in those tombs, for the people believed that after their deaths their souls would go to the other wourld and live there as the living do on earth. So a whole set of daily utensils was usually placed in side each tomb for the dead to use.

The burial objects include bowls, plates, bottles and some other cooking vessels. There were three or four pieces of pottery vessels in each tomb. It's noticeable that people at that time seldom used tools and weapons as their burial objects. It's obvious that tools and weapons were special concepts for the people in those days.

Burying the dead was one of the major practices prevailed at the time of Banpo. First they would place the remains of the dead in a certain place and waited for the time when the flesh became decayed and the they collected the bones and placed them inside the tombs with their head facing the west, the bones of the other parts of their bodies below their heads. The way of collecting bones was known as"washing bones burying method. "

Reburying the dead was probably derived from the belief

that only when the flesh got decayed could their souls go to the other world, for the people thought their flesh and blood belonged to the world. The ethnological data suggests that it would take a couple of months and even lonegr time and to have the dead reburied. Today the same practice still exists in China's Guangdong, Fujjan and Taiwan provinces.

There were seven tombs containing the dead with their chests and faces and their hands laying straight at their waists. Few burial objects were unearthed in those tombs, In many other parts of the world, such as India, central Asia, America and Hokkaido in Japan the peoples buried the dead the same way as they Banpo people did, although at different times and in different places. Wasn't it amazing? But why the Banpo people did that is still unknown to us. However, in some backward tribes, the chiefs, priests,and those killed by lightning who were died accidentally were buried in different ways.

There were only four tombs containing the dead with their bodies bent. It is that burying the dead with their bodies bent was for restoration of the embryo status in the wombs. Now you can understand why they were buried in that way. Others held that the dead was tied up for preventing the living from being hurt by the souls of the dead.

There were two typical joined tombs at Banpo. One contains the remains of male of 40—50, with an average height of 1. 70 m. The other contains those of female of 15——25,with an average height of 1. 60 m.

The mentioning of joint tombs reminds us of the Banpo people's attitute toward their marriage. You know, in those days every adult had a spouse (rather than a husband or a wife). Neighther side was dominated by the other. Therefore their sexual relations were loose. This is because both sides was independent economically. That is to say that both sides worked in their own clan community. They just lived together when they thought it was necessary. No brothers and sisters of the same clan were allowed to marry to each other. The adult men should go out to look for their spouses in he other clans. After the men deaths, they had to be buried in the cemetery of the clan community where they were born. According to the usual practice, they were not allowed to be buried with their own sisters. At the same time, the dead women were not allowed to be buried with their brothers, either. That's why the dead men and women were never buried together at Banpo. In those joint tombs the men and the women were buried separately once for all, because they belonged to the same generation or the interval of their deaths were not very long.

In the past the same custom was popular among the Dong people in China. Instead of burying the dead right after their deaths, they would put their remains in coffins and place them somewhere near their village. When someone else of the same village died, an auspicious day wooould be chosen by the living and then they would be buried in the same tomb, if they happened to be born in the same year and of the same generation. The above cases have thrown light on the joint burying practice. Those who were jointly buried not only belonged to the same generation but also born in the same year. The practice was associated with primitive religious ideas. The people believed that the brothers and sisters who were born in the same year should go to the other world in the same year. That's why in those days someone would be to accompany another person's death.

In the Banpo tombs many of the burial objects were broken purposely. But why? This is because the Banpo people thought that everything in the other world was opposite to that on earth. Only when they brake them, could the dead accept them complete things. We can see that the Banpo people already had complicated ideas about the mortal world and the other world. There must be more profound meanings regarding the burial custom at Banpo which require more intensive studies in the future.

几步之遥，就能体验六千年前的远古生活
一日之内，便可饱览女权社会的文化景观
古朴古久　粗犷粗放　原始原味　野情野趣

西安半坡母系氏族村简介

　　西安半坡母系氏族村是国内第一个表现人类母系氏族社会，荟萃黄河流域远古艺术、民俗风情和民居田园于一体的大型渡假游乐园。

　　西安半坡母系氏族村由香港新勇（中国）投资有限公司与西安半坡博物馆合作投资复原，座落在西安东郊风光秀丽的浐河之畔、白鹿原下，紧毗蜚誉中外的半坡村遗址大厅，占地约33000平方米。

　　西安半坡母系氏族村以积极保护遗址为前提，根据考古发掘的珍贵资料将遗址从地下搬到地上，从而达到丰富半坡博物馆内函，弘扬华夏悠久历史文化之目的，并发挥文物优势，为古城旅游业增添新的旅游景点。

　　游客在村落里，除可满足访古猎奇、娱乐休

息等旅游动机外,还可随时欣赏和参与反映半坡先民生产、生活和爱情的歌舞节目,以及远古器具和工艺纪念品的制作表演,品尝别具特色的半坡景宴、猎宴和野味快餐。另外,您还可在中心大房子、庆典广场和聚欢部落中逍遥观赏村内首批推出的远古的回声、史前服饰表演、原始角斗和娱乐等丰富有趣的活动,亲身体验史前社会粗犷的风土人情和浓厚的原始韵味。

徜徉村中,伴着古悠动听的陶乐之声,您还可以观赏到时光通道、森林古途、板桥观景、复原村、浐河渔趣、狩猎白鹿原、母腹洞穴、半坡别墅、陶山古韵等十多处景观。夜幕降临,人们集聚在庆典广场,可以纵情欣赏和参与古朴典雅、隆重吉祥又充满野趣百人大祭祀和"半坡之夜"大狂欢活动,使您在欢乐的气氛中,充分领略中华民族渊源流长,多姿多彩的文化底蕴。

西安半坡母系氏族村简介
INTRODUCTION TO BANPO MA-TRIARCHAL CLAN VILLAGE, XIAN

Banpo Matriarchal Clan Village, Xian, is the only original remains of a matriarchal clan in the country, mirroring the arts, custom, housing and gardening of the antique native in the Yellow River Valley. It is the place to pass your holidays.

Joint — ventured by Xinyong (China) Investment Co. Ltd. HongKong, and Banpo Museum, Xian, Banpo Matriarchal Clan Village lies close to Banpo Remains Hall on the beautiful bank of Chan River at the foot of the Whitedeer Highland, covering up 33000 square meters.

Taking the priority of conserving the remains, the village is a full — scale representation of the rare relics unearthed so far to enrich the content of the Museum and demonstrate the long culture of the nation, making a new beauty spot in Xi'an, one of the ancient capitals.

In additon to discovering the origin of the nation and entertaining yourself in the Village, you can enjoy the farming, hunting and daily life of the ancient native, take part in their love and funeral ceremonies, try your hand in manufacturing ancient tools and souvenirs and have a taste of the unique Banpo dinners, barbecues and game snacks. Also, roaming through the tea—huts, the inns and the center park or among the merry — making clans, you can appreciate the pageant of ancient arts, the performance of prehistoric clothing, primitive wrestling, clan clubs and many other activities to experience the rough custom and remote pleasure in the prehistoric times.

Wandering in the Village, you can also go through the Time Channel, walk on the Ancient Road in Woods, pass the Log Bridge leading you to the Restored Village, fishing in Chan River, hunt on the Whitedeer Highland, go into the Cave in Mother Belly, then have a rest in Banpo villa and enjoy the rhyme in the Pottery Mount. Now, night falls and all the people gather in the Center Park, freely enjoying themselves and taking part in Banpo Night, a huge — scale merry — making, simple, elegant, grand and full of wild flavor. At this moment, you will sure realize the longstream of the Chinese and her profound culture.

Let us meet in Banpo Matriarchal Clan Village, Xian, in the Tourist Historic Site Year'94.

半坡母系氏族村

陶山古韵

上　浐河渔趣
中　饮食村一隅
下　半坡彩绘

复原村落

原始舞蹈

古陶埙演奏

百人大祭祀

原始竞技

摄影师

张学德

赵建刚

李润泉

武天合

白　强

（陕）新登字003号

责任编辑	范茂震	
装帧计设		
插　图	任国钧	刘小红
摄　影	张学德	赵建刚
	李润泉	武天合
	白　强	

半坡母系社会

赵文艺　宋　澎　编著

陕西人民美术出版社出版发行

（西安北大街131号）

新华书店经销　　汉中地区印刷厂印刷

850×1168毫米　32开本　3印张　8插页　58千字

1994年10月第1版　1994年10月第1次印刷

印数：1—5,000

ISBN—5368—0651—5/J·546